The Guide to America's

MICRO BREWED BEER

D1553856

by Colin T. Flynn and Randy DelFranco

**Illustration and Graphic Design by
Richard A. Creighton**

THE
GUIDE TO AMERICA'S
MICROBREWED BEER

Published by:

Rose Hill Enterprises
P.O. Box 1015
Washington, D.C. 20013-1015

ISBN 0-9640948-0-0

Printed in the United States of America.

The authors would greatly appreciate any information or comments from readers that would enhance future editions of this book.

To Kathy

—C.T.F.

To my mother, Frances, whose wit is inspirational.

—R.D.

CONTENTS

INTRODUCTION

Well, we're still standing.
After sampling, and in some cases over-
sampling, hundreds of the finest beers in
the world—American microbrewed beer—it's
now time to call them as we see them.

Americans are famous for their love of beer,
and as the microbrewing revival has blossomed
there's a whole lot more to love. However, as
ever more brands of beer began crowding the
supermarket shelves, like many we found it
increasingly difficult to keep the dizzying array of
selections straight. Without much more to go on
than a fancy label and a catchy name, we made a
misstep or two. We quickly found some beers to
be less than what we had hoped for. Let's face it,
premium beer usually comes with a premium
price tag, so blind experimentation can be a
rather expensive endeavor. Thus, the concept for
this guide was born.

Our objective in this guide is to provide the
beer drinking public with a brief take on
hundreds of brands of beer available on the
market today. Our reviews and ratings will
hopefully enable you to recognize that not all
beers are created equal. You will discover that
some brands are quite exceptional, while others
fall a little short. We hope you take this guide
along as a handy reference when checking out
the newest arrivals at the supermarket, liquor or
package store, or your local watering hole.

To understand the current renaissance in
American brewing, a brief history lesson is in
order. Prior to that dark chapter known as
Prohibition, hundreds of small breweries
flourished across the country. Most larger
communities had at least one brewery that

provided the surrounding region with a constant supply of freshly brewed barrels of beer. While the 21st Amendment forever brought an end to that bizarre time when having a glass of beer was a criminal act, the tradition of small breweries never recovered. During the ensuing decades, the American beer market became dominated by a few giant breweries that made beer with a mass audience in mind. Taste and freshness promptly became casualties of the new era.

Over the past decade or so, the American beer industry has gone back to the future. With the help of some visionary lawmakers, many state and local laws have been relaxed to make small breweries once again commercially viable. As high-spirited entrepreneurs entered the fray, they quickly realized that the public's long bottled up demand for more flavorful beer was poised to break loose. The result was an explosion in both the number of breweries setting up shop as well as the volume of their sales. In addition, local pride has reemerged as an important factor for many when selecting a beer. This has fostered fierce loyalties to the locally brewed brands and has given a greater sense of identity to the brewery's hometown. While the growth has indeed been astounding, we can all delight that there is no sign it's about to be tapped out anytime soon.

In industry parlance, a microbrewery is customarily defined as a brewery that produces less than 15,000 barrels of beer annually. In attempting to meet the demand for their product, many outfits that began as microbreweries quickly found themselves outstripping that traditional definition almost overnight. While small breweries are faced with capacity constraints that limit their potential growth, some have been able to take their growing pains in stride and increase output to match the public's appetite. Regardless of whether breweries qualify as micros, regionals, or specialty brewers, to the average consumer they are all quite tiny when compared to the handful of lumbering giants that still reign supreme. With that in mind and for the sake of simplicity, all the brands contained herein are considered microbrews. In short, you probably won't be seeing any of the beers we review pitched in a commercial during the next Super Bowl. Word of mouth, rather than huge ad campaigns, drives the microbrewing craze. We're just throwing our two cents in like everybody else.

You may ask yourself what qualifies two former college drinking buddies to review beer. Well, your guess is as good as ours. Actually, we wrote this book on the premise that beer is not about science or high art. Beer is beer. That is not to say that American microbrewers haven't succeeded beyond measure in developing extremely sophisticated brewing recipes that have resulted in a fabulous variety of beer tastes and styles. However, to average beer drinkers—and we proudly count ourselves among that not-so-exclusive group—beer is to be enjoyed as a refreshing respite from life's cares and concerns. It shouldn't be treated as if only the most sagacious among us were capable of detecting its particular qualities or inherent flaws. We recognize that beer tasting is highly subjective and your opinions may differ from ours. Therefore, we invite you to take our comments for what they're worth—nothing more, nothing less.

To the microbrewers of this country, who put their heart and soul into their product, we offer our praise and admiration. Each beer that we had the pleasure of sampling in our travels possesses its own special signature. Undoubtedly, this is due to the labor and dedication of the hundreds of microbrewers who are transforming the beer drinking habits of the nation.

Whether beer is your pastime or passion, we hope *The Guide to America's Microbrewed Beer* provides plenty of helpful information. If it provokes a chuckle or two, well, that's even better.

Colin T. Flynn

Randy DelFranco

The RATING SYSTEM

🪙 .... Definitely an acquired taste.

🪙🪙 .... A solid job, but you may be disappointed.

🪙🪙🪙 .... Shell out the dough and grab a six pack.

🪙🪙🪙🪙 .... Not perfection, but knocking on the door.

🪙🪙🪙🪙🪙 ..... Masterpiece territory. If you don't get your hands on it, you'll leave this planet unfulfilled.

The LINEUP

ABBEY TRAPPIST STYLE ALE

New Belgium Brewing Company, Inc.
350 Linden Street
Fort Collins, Colorado 80524
(303) 221-0524

Label Musings: Artistic sketch of a bald monk. The label fails to indicate whether holy water was used in the brewing process. Not a small detail to leave out.

Colin: While exotic flavors in beer tend to appeal to me, the grab bag of tastes in this offering is a bit overdone. You can't miss the hint of cloves in the aftertaste. Won't make you see the light. 🍺 ½

Randy: Break your vow of silence and tell all of your friends about this divine, ethereal fruity brew. It's not only for the religiously inclined. My prayers have been answered. 🍺🍺🍺

ABITA AMBER LAGER

Abita Brewing Co., Inc.
P.O. Box 762
Abita Springs, Louisiana 70420
(504) 893-3143

Label Musings: Artistic brown and tan label from the ragin' Cajuns of Louisiana.

Colin: The folks down South are famous for their hospitality, but to serve this brew wouldn't be in keeping with that tradition. If it's an amber you crave, you can find many brews made north of the Mason-Dixon Line to satisfy you. 🍺 ½

Randy: Mild, crisp amber. Not too heavy if you're looking to knock back a couple. Remember, of course, that knocking back a couple of ales could knock you out. Bully for the boys from the Bayou. 🍺🍺🍺

ABITA TURBO DOG

Abita Brewing Co., Inc.
P.O. Box 762
Abita Springs, Louisiana 70420
(504) 893-3143

Label Musings: Short, stout bottle with yellow lettering on black background. Those Cajuns sure have style.

Colin: Not fit for man or beast. I thought dogs were supposed to be man's best friend. That maxim flies out the window with this one. Beware of Dog. Turbo Dog that is. 🍺

Randy: This is a porter, which is not stated on the label, unless "Turbo Dog" means as much in Creole. Not a bad porter with a sweet and burnt flavor, but why not tell people? There's no way to determine what you're getting until it's opened. I guess that's our job. 🍺🍺

ALASKAN AMBER BEER

Alaskan Brewing & Bottling Co.
5429 Shaune Drive
Juneau, Alaska 99801
(907) 780-5866

Label Musings: Fishing trawler must be heading out for those tasty Pacific salmon. Way up there, it's either green in the summer or white the rest of the year.

Colin: This Dusseldorf-style Alt beer is a solid, worthy effort from the folks up in the 49th state, but not exactly a triumph. All in all, it's tasty but very predictable. You should expose yourself to some Northern delights. 🍺🍺 ¹/₂

Randy: You don't have to fly, boat or swim up to Alaska for this fine, satisfying amber beer, which hopefully will be available soon outside the Pacific Northwest. If you're up in Juneau, stop off in one of the many saloons. I recommend the free peanuts at the Red Dog Saloon. Throw the shells on the floor. 🍺🍺🍺 ¹/₂

ALASKAN PALE ALE

Alaskan Brewing & Bottling Co.
5429 Shaune Drive
Juneau, Alaska 99801
(907) 780-5866

Label Musings: Blue ice streaming from an ancient glacier. The Aurora Borealis is displayed. The North Country's astounding beauty is well captured on this sharp label.

Colin: Distinctive flavor but not much kick. I would have expected a feistier beer from the folks on the northern frontier. Pretty tame stuff, but hardly unpleasant. However, it may get Maggie and Joel started. 🍺🍺 1/2

Randy: Easy and breezy like the fun folks in and around landlocked Juneau. If you've ever been up there, you know how important "social" drinking is. And this certainly measures up. 🍺🍺🍺

ALIMONY ALE

Buffalo Bill's Brewery
1082 B Street
Hayward, California 94541
(510) 886-9823

Label Musings: The label displays an old-fashioned, cartoon-style loud-mouth yelping, "The Bitterest Brew in America." No wonder his wife flew the coop.

Colin: Pure gimmickry. This ale is destined to become the official beer of dead-beat dads. If your sense of humor is on the morbid side, send a case over to a pal who has just been taken to the cleaners in family court. To everyone else, it's likely to hit a raw nerve. Unless you want to cheer up a recently divorced friend, pass this one by. 🍺🍺

Randy: It is not the "bitterest brew in America," but who cares. This is a flavorful, even-tasting, bitter ale that is quite nice. As expected, it has a big head. I think the bitter dude on the label should lose the attitude. 🍺🍺🍺

ANCHOR LIBERTY ALE

Anchor Brewing Co.
1705 Mariposa Street
San Francisco, California 94107
(415) 863-8350

Label Musings: The wingspan of an American eagle behind a gold anchor. A classic label from a classy brewery. Label states it's one of the nation's smallest breweries. It won't be for long.

Colin: While our nation's founding documents proclaim that all men are created equal, that credo does not apply to ales. They all must earn their stripes and Liberty Ale certainly does just that. You'll be struck at first by its rich, creamy head (pour this one in a glass, it'll be worth the trouble). The taste is stable and satisfying. It deserves your respect and patronage. 🍺🍺🍺 ¹/₂

Randy: Thick head combined with a robust flavor and lots of malted barley. While aging, "dry hopping" techniques are used until the fermentation process is complete. Good, but not the best of the Anchor family. 🍺🍺🍺

ANCHOR OUR SPECIAL ALE

Anchor Brewing Co.
1705 Mariposa Street
San Francisco, California 94107
(415) 863-8350

Label Musings: A sketch of the Malus pumila (translation: a big, old tree) and a bizarre explanation about the significance of trees to life accent this unique label. The tree on the label as well as the recipe changes annually so save a few as heirlooms.

Colin: A very tasty ale indeed. The usual bite of an ale is replaced with zesty spice in this seasonal offering. A special treat if you're lucky enough to find it. 🍺🍺🍺🍺

Randy: This stout-like ale has lots of spicy flavor. Give it a try, but you'll probably stop after just one. Find a shade tree and contemplate the significance of beer to life. 🍺🍺🍺

ANCHOR PORTER

Anchor Brewing Co.
1705 Mariposa Street
San Francisco, California 94107
(415) 863-8350

Label Musings: One of the best labels out there, on a distinctly shaped squat bottle. The patriotic aura and script lettering lend an antique air.

Colin: Ample, roasted malt taste comes through loud and clear. If you have a hankering for a stout, take it down a notch and give this one by the Frisco pros a try instead. 🍺🍺🍺

Randy: The label states that the brew is "aesthetically pleasing and wholly superior in every respect." Such claims are brash and bold and so is the beer. Dark with an abundant head, it's full of flavor and taste. A masterful job. 🍺🍺🍺🍺

ANCHOR STEAM

Anchor Brewing Co.
1705 Mariposa Street
San Francisco, California 94107
(415) 863-8350

Label Musings: The old-fashioned blue anchor over a sunny background makes us think of Fisherman's Wharf. The bottle is distinctly rounded and stocky (remind you of any beer drinkers you know?).

Colin: An esteemed beverage if ever there was one. An old-timer by microbrew standards, one taste and you'll instantly appreciate this classic. It has a complete and full-flavored effect. As long as The Big One doesn't hit the Bay Area, this beer will be around forever. I'd consider making a break from Alcatraz for a six-pack. 🍺🍺🍺🍺

Randy: It has a huge head and a copious amber flavor. Seems like many years of brewing have gotten this one close to perfection. If I'm out on the town, I could drink this all night. If you're looking for a seismic event, put away a six-pack of this brewski. It'll make the earth move under your feet. 🍺🍺🍺🍺 ¹/₂

AUGSBURGER GOLDEN

The Stroh Brewery Company
100 River Place
Detroit, Michigan 48207
(313) 446-2000

Label Musings: We know it's from Stroh's (not exactly a tiny outfit), but it's packaged and marketed as a microbrew, so we threw it in. It has a well-designed, German-style, green and gold label.

Colin: While the taste is far from disagreeable, the beer was obviously brewed with the lowest common denominator in mind (and you know who you are). It succeeds on its own modest terms, the phony German accents and overtones notwithstanding. 🍺🍺

Randy: Although it is smooth and even, it lacks the flavor of many other ales. No standout here, but you won't go wrong as it is solid and consistent. 🍺🍺 ¹/₂

BADERBRAU BOCK BEER

Pavichevich Brewing Co.
383 Romans Road
Elmhurst, Illinois 60126
(708) 617-5252

Label Musings: Stylish gold stripe with green and black scheme. At least there's no goat's head, an all-too-common trademark of bock labels. For you stock market gamblers, the NASDAQ symbol is "BRAU." You should read our review before you place your bet.

Colin: You may want to invest for some capital gains. If you can't resist hot fudge sundaes, you'll love this chocolaty bock. Hold the whipped cream and cherry, this brew is dessert enough. 🍺🍺🍺

Randy: The label instructs you to pour vigorously and serve at 55 degrees. Thanks for the tip. This creamy-headed, smooth bock is impressive indeed. I know some hearty Chicagoans who love throwin' these babies back. 🍺🍺🍺 ¹/₂

BADERBRAU PILSENER BEER

Pavichevich Brewing Co.
383 Romans Road
Elmhurst, Illinois 60126
(708) 617-5252

Label Musings: A German name and a label to match. Now all we need is an oom-pah band and some stein-wielding frauleins.

Colin: This is not an exceptional beer. It has an adequate flavor, though it lacks a smooth finish. Its dull, cloudy color matches its forgettable taste. A true underachiever. 🍺 ½

Randy: Malty, barley flavor overwhelms this dark pilsner. Its fresh taste makes you think it came right out of the copper kettle, which it probably did. Hearty enough for Ditka. 🍺🍺 ½

BALLANTINE INDIA PALE ALE

Falstaff Brewing Corp.
P.O. Box 926
Fort Wayne, Indiana 46801
(219) 424-7232

Label Musings: A gold clipper ship accented by the old Ballantine symbol. You remember—the thing that looks like a pretzel. Don't forget to look under the bottle cap.

Colin: One of the better pale ales out there. A robust taste is unhindered by the usual bite. To its detriment, what bitterness there is lingers long after you swallow. Overall, a pleasant drinking experience. 🍺🍺🍺 ½

Randy: The history of pale ale is described as having been "Discovered in 1824—purely by chance—when a keg of rare ale was opened between England and Calcutta...." These brewers have been around almost as long as India pale ale. The red color shows through the green bottle. It's a wonderful, flavor-packed brew. The old guys have still got it. 🍺🍺🍺🍺

BALLARD BITTER PALE ALE

The Redhook Ale Brewery
3400 Phinney Avenue North
Seattle, Washington 98103
(206) 548-8000

Label Musings: The brewery is located in Seattle's historic Fremont Trolley Barn. The label has portraits of old-fashioned (circa 1884-1941) trolley men. I love that mustache on A.A. Massoni. "Ya sure, ya betcha."

Colin: It lives up to its name. Bitter to a fault. If you have a penchant for self-inflicted wounds, be my guest. Otherwise, steer clear. 🍺 ¹/₂

Randy: Very bitter and disagreeable. Those trolley old-timers must have been a hearty (or masochistic) lot. Do you want the trolley driver drinking? 🍺 ¹/₂

BANKS BEER

Banks Brewery Ltd.
Cincinnati, Ohio 45214

Label Musings: Like so many labels, this one prominently displays a clipper ship. Evokes a small brewery's "we-don't-want-to-spend-a-lot-on-the-label" attitude. We can respect that. The painted, long-neck bottle is definitely a plus.

Colin: This one didn't win me over. The brewery is supervised by the Banks group from Guyana. What's that? You say you're unfamiliar with that beer mecca? I believe it's in South America. Hey, geography was never my strong suit. 🍺 ¹/₂

Randy: This beer has a crisp, light, "brewery-fresh" (as the label boasts) flavor. Frankly, it tastes like the stuff you get on the tours of the big breweries. The hoppy flavor is enjoyable, but doesn't set it apart. 🍺🍺 ¹/₂

BELK'S BITTER ALE

Anderson Valley Brewing Co.
P.O. Box 505
Boonville, California 95415
(707) 895-2337

Label Musings: It comes from a land "beyond the Baldies, northeast of Boonville." Huh? Actually, it's brewed in Mendocino County, California. There isn't a lone figure in the pastoral setting, but if you look closely you can make out a deer in the distance. One shot.

Colin: If you possess an ornery temperament, or want to acquire one, partake in this bitter brew. If you're not mad at the world, then stay clear. I've heard of drowning your sorrows in a mug of beer, but this one will put a frown on even the most cheerful mugs. Don't drink it; be happy. 🍺

Randy: OK, it's extremely bitter. If that was their objective, they have succeeded beyond their wildest dreams. So does that mean they should get high marks? I say no, because the average beer drinker isn't likely to go for it. However, if you love bitter ale, you may have found your ideal bottle of brew. 🍺 ½

BERGHOFF BEER

Berghoff-Huber Brewing Co., Ltd.
P.O. Box 277, 1208 14th Avenue
Monroe, Wisconsin 53566
(608) 325-3191

Label Musings: Green bottle with definite German accents including a German eagle. Hey, this ain't the Fatherland.

Colin: For all you import lovers who want to keep profits stateside, this is your American-brewed alternative. A hint of bite and a full taste provide a quintessentially European beer experience. 🍺🍺🍺 ½

Randy: This crisp, resplendent, golden Dortmunder-style brew is easy-going. It would be perfect with a hot dog, kraut and brown mustard. Ooh, I'm hungry. 🍺🍺🍺 ½

BERGHOFF BOCK

Berghoff-Huber Brewing Co., Ltd.
P.O. Box 277
1208 14th Avenue
Monroe, Wisconsin 53566
(608) 325-3191

Label Musings: Black and copper label with Berghoff signature and that ever-present symbol for bock beer: a ram.

Colin: I've heard of double bocks, but this one is a triple bocker if you ask me. Extremely dark and pungent, it easily defines the outer edge of the bock family. A black sheep perhaps? 🍺🍺🍺

Randy: Dark and chocolaty, with a hint of burnt aftertaste. It's definitely a "one-is-enough" sort of beer. Flavorful, but that lingering aftertaste kept me up at night. Pass the decaf. 🍺 ½

BICYCLE APRICOT STONE

Evansville Brewing Co.
1301 West Lloyd Expwy.
Evansville, Indiana 47710
(812) 425-7101

Label Musings: Tequila sunrise with intense bicycle riders. We're not sure why it's called "BICYCLE," but that's another story.

Colin: I think the wine cooler crowd—if they're still around—may join the micro craze after tasting this "beer." I can see how the aerobics gang might latch on to this fruity, light beverage. But if you don't count yourself among that ilk, don't shame yourself. 🍺🍺

Randy: The wine cooler industry has nothing to fear. Wine can be sweetened up, but I think most would agree it doesn't quite work the same way for beer. 🍺 ½

BICYCLE MISTY LIME

Evansville Brewing Co.
1301 West Lloyd Expwy.
Evansville, Indiana 47710
(812) 425-7101

Label Musings: Aquamarine, green and yellow
background for our biker pals.

Colin: I've heard of the uncola, but this may very
well be the unbeer. Lemon-lime beer? I don't think
so. Don't cave to the peer pressure of the fad follow-
ers. Just say no.

Randy: Our job is to inform you so that you can
sample the best of microbrews and avoid the worst.
Here we have a perfect case in point. Avoid this.
C'mon guys, lime beer? One look at this greenish,
murky broth and a shiver went up my spine. My
opinion didn't improve once I took a gulp. 1/2

BICYCLE VERIBERRY

Evansville Brewing Co.
1301 West Lloyd Expwy.
Evansville, Indiana 47710
(812) 425-7101

Label Musings: Those Tour de France guys on a
berry watercolor background. Believe it or not, this is
sold in the beer section.

Colin: To beer purists, it's sure to be dead in the
water. To each his own, but in this case try to avoid
being sucked in by the novelty. It'll wear off after the
first sip.

Randy: Did you ever have great cherry soda? Well,
spike it with your favorite brew and ruin both. Strictly
for the faddist. Veribad.

BLACKHOOK PORTER

The Redhook Ale Brewery
3400 Phinney Avenue North
Seattle, Washington 98103
(206) 548-8000

Label Musings: Odd, off-beat, black label with what looks like a cross between a directional signal and a gender symbol. Confusing.

Colin: This porter has a capricious flavor. It approaches stout with its cocoa color and creamy consistency, yet it lacks that mighty flavor. Fascinating, but flighty. 🍺🍺 ½

Randy: A wonderful, London-style porter: sweet and mysterious. I guess the crazy label is meant to baffle. Porter is the predecessor to stout. In fact, the original name of stout was stout porter. This brew is stout-like in its inexhaustible richness. I'm hooked. 🍺🍺🍺🍺

BLACKWELL STOUT

The New Haven Brewing Company
458 Grand Avenue
New Haven, Connecticut 06513
(203) 772-2739

Label Musings: Dog lovers will adore the portrait of the loyal black Labrador on the label. It'll surely warm your heart. You'll also get a kick out of the paw print on the bottle cap.

Colin: Admittedly, I'm not a stout fan, but this forceful yet creamy brew may prompt me to join the ranks. For all those prone to knee-jerk rejections of stout, this just might be the perfect introduction. 🍺🍺🍺 ½

Randy: This coffee-like stout is as dark as the Labrador on the label. Don't drink it late at night unless you need to stay awake. I took milk and two sugars with mine. It is smooth and sweet; somewhat like Guinness, to which this all-American compares favorably. 🍺🍺🍺 ½

BLIZZARD BOCK

The Buffalo Brewing Company
1830 Abbott Road
Buffalo, New York 14218
(716) 828-0004

Label Musings: Snow-bound buffalo stuck in a purple blizzard. It doesn't look like he's gonna make it. Poor guy. At least there's no goat.

Colin: Poor visibility from that storm may have grounded this bock. All the bock elements are present, but the overall effect left me feeling adrift. 🍺🍺

Randy: Almost root beer-like sweetness. The light bock flavor goes down easily. My only complaint would be that it's too light. I can't say the same for the beast on the label. 🍺🍺 ½

BLUEBONNET PREMIUM BEER

Texas Brewing Company, Inc.
703 McKinney Avenue
Dallas, Texas 75202
(214) 871-7990

Label Musings: This beer gets its name from the Texas state flower, which adorns the label. Hey, state pride certainly has its rightful place, but there's something about a flower on a bottle of brewski that doesn't sit well with us. Higher marks for the yellow bottle cap that comes complete with a horseshoe on a snazzy blue and gold background.

Colin: I would expect a little more swagger from the good ol' boys down in Big D. It is refreshing and light. Under the sweltering Texas sun, I guess that counts for something. 🍺🍺

Randy: While full of flavor for a light lager, this isn't a taste I go for. A hint of sour mash is unmistakable. If Texans want an outlet to show off their state pride, they need look no further than their legendary Cowboys. This beer isn't worthy enough for pre-game tailgating. 🍺 ½

BOSTON LIGHTSHIP

Boston Beer Company
30 Germania Street
Boston, Massachusetts 02130
(617) 522-3400

Label Musings: The Megan Charles fights its way through the mighty Atlantic. Yea, it's another ship, but one of the best we've seen. The usual portrait of Samuel Adams is missing. Is he below deck, or lost at sea?

Colin: The makers of the Sam Adams brands were bound to hit the market with a light beer entry. However, I expected a less conventional offering from them. Even legends in their own time can occasionally fall short of their usual lofty standards. 🍺🍺

Randy: Brewmaster Jimmy Koch states that there are no artificial means used in reducing the calories of this brew. That's fine, but the flavor went out with the calories. Merely hoppy water doesn't float my boat. 🍺

BRECKENRIDGE AVALANCHE

Breckenridge Brewery
2220 Blake Street
Denver, Colorado 80205
(303) 297-3644

Label Musings: There's no avalanche. Just a sleepy little town. It certainly doesn't remind us of Breckenridge, Colorado—a hoppin' ski town.

Colin: If your leg's in a cast and you're stuck in the lodge, make yourself comfortable with this hefty brew. Not much nuance here, just blunt, hard-nosed taste. Remember, this is the pick only if you're not going anywhere for a while. Otherwise, lay off. It's double black diamond time with this stuff. 🍺🍺🍺 1/2

Randy: This is a strong, insolent and tasty amber ale that is also surprisingly smooth. They should sell this stuff at Colorado Rockies home games; Adolph Coors be damned. Yet, somehow, I don't think he would appreciate that. 🍺🍺🍺

BRECKENRIDGE MOUNTAIN WHEAT

Breckenridge Brewery
2220 Blake Street
Denver, Colorado 80205
(303) 297-3644

Label Musings: Black print on an oatmeal background. This plain label exhibits a sketch of a quaint ski town.

Colin: The perfect beer for an apres-ski happy hour. Smooth and light, its delicate flavor will help you mellow out after a long day on the slopes. Of course, it'll have the same effect if you're partial to less taxing pastimes, like watching the tube.

Randy: The label describes how this brew was founded on the slopes of Breckenridge by some dude named Richard. This wheat beer is fruitier and lighter than most, however, it doesn't have that wheaty flavor that I adore. It's like a slalom skier who missed a gate.

BRECKENRIDGE OATMEAL STOUT

Breckenridge Brewery
2220 Blake Street
Denver, Colorado 80205
(303) 297-3644

Label Musings: Ginger-colored version of standard Breckenridge label scheme.

Colin: Only for those with a stout constitution and a love affair with oatmeal—not a very large group, I presume. High marks for technical merit, lower ones for artistic impression. Hey, beer tasting is a very subjective endeavor.

Randy: On the crowded slopes of Breckenridge, I'm sure you could find many who would swear by the stuff. As I'm swooshing downhill, I'd like something lighter in me. I suggest you refrain from sampling this hearty stout before hitting the moguls.

BRIDGEPORT BLUE HERON PALE ALE

Bridgeport Brewing Company
1313 N.W. Marshall
Portland, Oregon 97209
(503) 241-7179

Label Musings: The majestic blue heron is eye-catching. Wading in a creek, it looks larger than life. That ain't no duck.

Colin: There's no glory in this brew. It has a mediocre, overripe taste that falters. Doesn't go down easily. This heron laid an egg. 🍺 ½

Randy: The haughty stork couldn't be proud of this amber brew's tepid and inconsistent taste. Maybe the bird should lay off the baby deliveries and spend some more time in the brewery. Fly on by. 🍺

BRIDGEPORT COHO PACIFIC LIGHT ALE

Bridgeport Brewing Company
1313 N.W. Marshall
Portland, Oregon 97209
(503) 241-7179

Label Musings: It's a jumper! This Coho salmon is a prize catch and I'd bet he would be pretty tasty with some cream cheese on a bagel.

Colin: A very interesting taste, but never quite gets its footing. No staying power. This fish has already swum upstream. 🍺🍺

Randy: Light with a bountiful, fruity flavor and an amber color. Quite an achievement for a light ale. This brew is bound to spawn imitations. 🍺🍺🍺

BROOKLYN BROWN DARK ALE

Brooklyn Brewery
118 North Eleventh Street
Brooklyn, New York 11211
(718) 486-7422

Label Musings: "All-American" says it all. Brown and gold in big lettering. These New Yorkers talk a big game, but they also walk the walk.

Colin: Brown bottle, brown label, brown beer. This street-fightin' power puncher challenges you with its potent flavor. If you're looking for a knock-down, drag-out brew, I recommend it. 🍺🍺🍺🍺

Randy: The Boys of Summer would be proud of this slightly sweet dark ale. No bitterness, no overwhelming bite. It goes down easy. Yo, this is a mint brewski. Crown these brewmasters the kings of Kings. Kings County, that is. 🍺🍺🍺🍺 ½

BROOKLYN LAGER

Brooklyn Brewery
118 North Eleventh Street
Brooklyn, New York 11211
(718) 486-7422

Label Musings: Snazzy green, black and gold label, with a prominent "B" that may stand for "Brooklyn" or "beer" or "bravo." The six-pack holder explains that it's all-barley malt, aged ("lagered") for 6 to 8 weeks, "dry-hopped" using extra hops, and naturally carbonated ("krausened") during an additional round of fermentation.

Colin: Resolute and hearty like the folks who hail from the Big Apple's largest borough. Brooklyn may have lost the Dodgers back in '57, but at least now they have this dandy lager they can call their own. All in all, not a bad trade. 🍺🍺🍺 ½

Randy: This beer will put Brooklyn back on the map. I'm so damn proud that this fine lager is brewed in my hometown. Did you say that I might be biased? Not! This is a smooth, hearty drinking beer with a plucky, woody kick. After a six-pack, I may even forgive Walter O'Malley. But I doubt it. 🍺🍺🍺🍺 ½

BUFFALO LAGER

The Buffalo Brewing Company
1830 Abbott Road
Lackawanna, New York 14218
(716) 828-0004

Label Musings: Big, beefy buffalo depicted on a copper background.

Colin: This beer is apparently brewed with buffalos, oxen and other hefty members of the animal kingdom in mind. What else could explain the insufferable taste? Surely it must be in stock at the local feed store.

Randy: Easy enough going down, but a bitter aftertaste. Far from pleasing. I'm here to warn you, this buffalo has gone rogue. Everybody run! 1/2

BUNKERHILL LAGER

Bunkerhill Brewing Co.
c/o The Lion Inc.
700 North Pennsylvania Avenue
Wilkes-Barre, Pennsylvania 18705
(717) 823-8801

Label Musings: Modern art number with geometric designs and gold foil on the neck. Looks like an import. The packaging doesn't seem fitting for a beer named Bunkerhill. Plus, the brewery isn't even in Beantown. What's going on here?

Colin: A rather uninspired bottle of beer. A meek taste marks this forgettable brew. Regardless of what happened at the Battle of Bunker Hill, what's in the bottle doesn't taste like sweet victory. 1/2

Randy: More like the Boston Massacre. Full of hops. Tastes like their recipe could use a little work. If you love hops, go for it, but it hops straight up.

CAPITAL GARTEN BRAU

Capital Brewery Co. Inc.
P.O. Box 620185
Middleton, Wisconsin 53562
(608) 836-7100

Label Musings: Declares "Wisconsin—Beer Capital of the World." There's a scene of a capitol building. Is that Madison or D.C. or that mythical "Beer Capitol Building"?

Colin: Everybody is fighting over where the beer capital is. I'll tell you where it is. It's your favorite pub; the one within walking distance. As for this beer, it is too light to grab your attention. 🍺 ½

Randy: You can taste the hops in this pilsner. It's quite refreshing and not heavy. For those hot, humid August days. It's not for cheeseheads only. 🍺🍺 ½

CATAMOUNT AMBER

Catamount Brewing Company
58 South Main Street
P.O. Box 457
White River Junction, Vermont 05001
(802) 296-2248

Label Musings: The bronze background and mountain lion are catchy. They lead you to expect a ferocious brew.

Colin: I didn't know there were many mountain lions in the Granite State. This one is feisty and rough around the edges. While it is teeming with flavor, I was disappointed with the overall effect. 🍺🍺

Randy: This beer reminded me of the taste you get when you chew gum too long. It is sour and bitter. When I drink beer, I want to enjoy it. In my opinion, drinking this stuff isn't enjoyable. 🍺

CATAMOUNT CHRISTMAS ALE

Catamount Brewing Company
58 South Main Street
P.O. Box 457
White River Junction, Vermont 05001
(802) 296-2248

Label Musings: Looks like a cheap Christmas card. Maybe they should enlist some of the masters over at Hallmark to spruce it up. Just a thought.

Colin: Where's the Christmas spirit? No zest and no spice. There are plenty of other specialty beers out there that will likely strike you as more festive. However, a six-pack under the tree would be a welcome gift from St. Nick. I'm tired of getting neckties. 🍺🍺 ¹/₂

Randy: There's tons of flavor in this delectable ale. Put this on the table with that Christmas goose. One of these and ol' Ebeneezer Scrooge wouldn't have needed those ghosts to cheer him up. 🍺🍺🍺 ¹/₂

CATAMOUNT GOLD

Catamount Brewing Company
58 South Main Street
P.O. Box 457
White River Junction, Vermont 05001
(802) 296-2248

Label Musings: Gold background for the Catamount kitty. The sketch of the big cat on the bottlecap is a keeper.

Colin: You are sure to enjoy this exceptional beer. Clean, crisp and clear, this one delivers the goods. After sampling it, you'll fully appreciate why micros are taking over the USA. Big brand drinkers wake up and smell the Catamount Gold. 🍺🍺🍺🍺🍺

Randy: The pride of the North Country (as the label proclaims). This cat has a sharp bite. I had cat-scratch fever after a few sips. Mellow and light enough for a multi-beer night. 🍺🍺🍺🍺

CATAMOUNT PORTER

Catamount Brewing Company
58 South Main Street
P.O. Box 457
White River Junction, Vermont 05001
(802) 296-2248

Label Musings: The best of the Catamount labels. Dark and foreboding ambiance tells you you're about to encounter something different. Nifty red cap.

Colin: Far too rich for the average Joe or Jane. It's better you know that now than have the bulk of the six lie in the fridge ad infinitum. But porter fans will likely take notice. 🍺🍺🍺

Randy: George Washington loved porter beer and he went on to become the Father of our Country. See what good beer can do. Although porter-style beer once nearly vanished, it has been making a comeback in recent years. This is a fascinating lighter-than-stout beer with a bitter, burnt flavor. For all those new to porter, it provides a perfect primer. 🍺🍺🍺 ¹/₂

CELIS GOLDEN

Celis Brewery
2431 Forbes Drive
Austin, Texas 78754
(512) 835-0884

Label Musings: The label explains that it's Hill Country brew from Texas, and shows a bunch of confused hillbillies mixing stuff in a huge, wooden vat surrounded by some European-looking symbols. Weird.

Colin: It's golden alright, but not quite 24 carat. It has character and crispness with no bitterness. Most certainly, it is a quality brew. Although not the stuff of legends, I was quite satisfied. 🍺🍺🍺 ¹/₂

Randy: Smooth! This is a tremendous achievement for American brewing. If I were wearing a hat, I'd tip it to Pierre Celis for his magnificent, light golden lager. It's got what most Americans would consider a European taste. This is the best of Europe in the good ol' U.S. of A. It's Medal of Honor time. 🍺🍺🍺🍺🍺

CELIS GRAND CRU

Celis Brewery
2431 Forbes Drive
Austin, Texas 78754
(512) 835-0884

Label Musings: Thankfully, the only Celis label without those hillbillies. But why in the world did they put a bust of a Greek goddess on it instead? It's anybody's guess, but I'm sure Mr. Celis knows its special meaning.

Colin: Touts itself as a "Hill Country Ale." After a couple of sips, you'll want to head for the hills yourself. Harsh, hostile and downright uncivilized. Did I mention it is potent? Oof! 🍺 ½

Randy: "And up from the ground came a bubblin' brew." No, it doesn't taste like Texas tea, but it does taste strangely like a wheat beer. I have a soft spot for wheat beer flavor, so I took a likin' to it. 🍺🍺🍺

CELIS PALE BOCK

Celis Brewery
2431 Forbes Drive
Austin, Texas 78754
(512) 835-0884

Label Musings: Those crazy hill folk don't look like world class brewmasters to us. They look like they should be out skinnin' raccoons.

Colin: What a wonderful idea. Bring bock down a notch to make it more enticing to the more cautious among us. It worked beautifully. Don't serve this bock only in the spring; it's a year-round winner.
🍺🍺🍺🍺

Randy: Pale ale, pale bock. Actually, this brew pales in comparison to other bocks. Also, where the hell is the goat on the label? Are they sure it's a bock beer?
🍺🍺

CELIS WHITE

Celis Brewery
2431 Forbes Drive
Austin, Texas 78754
(512) 838-0884

Label Musings: Gold and cream color scheme looks classy, but it's marred by the prominent display of those baffled mountain men. According to the brewers, white beer brewing disappeared with the closing of the last brewery of its kind in Hoegaarden, Belgium in 1957. Pierre came to America in 1990 with his daughter Christine and together they carry on this brewing tradition.

Colin: I think somebody switched the labels because I could have sworn I drank a white wine spritzer. Much too fruity for my palate. On those sweltering summer days, stick to wine coolers if you must, or better yet, choose a more satisfying wheat beer. 🍺🍺 ¹/₂

Randy: Wheatier than Wheaties. If you're from the wheat belt or live for wheat, you've found Valhalla. For those of you who haven't tried wheat beer, this slightly overdone, cloudy specimen may spoil others for you. 🍺🍺🍺 ¹/₂

CHICAGO'S HEARTLAND WEISS

Chicago Brewing Co.
1830 North Besly Court
Chicago, Illinois 60622
(312) 252-2739

Label Musings: The skyline of the Windy City at sunset. The gold and beige label has a wheaty frame. This brewery uses a flash pasteurization process which keeps the beer fresher longer.

Colin: The label informs us that in the late 1800s, German immigrants J. Jerusalem and Ernst Funk established themselves with the "aid of the resources of the rich, grain-producing farms of Illinois." Thanks to those marvelous pioneers, we have this wonderful weiss beer available beyond the heartland. 🍺🍺🍺🍺

Randy: The tired, poor and huddled masses yearning to breathe free certainly have panned out for us! Now, we have the best tried and true German brewing techniques to make our beer right here at home. Have this spunky weiss beer with a big, soft, salty pretzel and mustard. Mmmmm! 🍺🍺🍺🍺 ¹/₂

CHICAGO'S LEGACY LAGER

Chicago Brewing Co.
1830 North Besly Court
Chicago, Illinois 60622
(312) 252-2739

Label Musings: Burnt orange, with lots of wheat and hops. This is the kind of stuff Al Capone and his cronies swilled and Elliott Ness did his damndest to confiscate. Hey, just who were the bad guys?

Colin: A roasted malt flavor creates a chocolate aftertaste. This is a formidable brew and earns high marks. I invite all premium beer lovers to sample this one. 🍺🍺🍺🍺

Randy: The tremendous hop flavor is almost criminal, but why would anyone want to outlaw this stuff? I'm glad I was born too late to suffer through the era of Prohibition. Carrie Nation R.I.P. 🍺🍺🍺🍺

CHICAGO'S LEGACY RED ALE

Chicago Brewing Co.
1830 North Besly Court
Chicago, Illinois 60622
(312) 252-2739

Label Musings: Colorful and artistic red backing with green ovals. It has a coat of arms with a harp, hops, clover and water tower. One of the best labels you'll find.

Colin: Chocolaty, and not semisweet either. Throw it in the microwave and you just might end up with hot cocoa. For chocoholics like me, that's not a bad thing. Otherwise, a solid brew, though probably not the beer of choice for happy hour. 🍺🍺🍺

Randy: The label states that the ghosts of 19th century brewers Richard Keeley and John Fortune are revived. This roasted flavor ale might be well above par technically, but I don't imagine many Cubs fans at Wrigley Field jumping over each other trying to reach a vendor for this one. 🍺🍺 1/2

CHIEF OSHKOSH

Midcoast Brewing Co.
35 Wisconsin Street
Oshkosh, Wisconsin 54902
(414) 236-3307

Label Musings: Half-naked Big Chief Oshkosh in enormous headdress posed before a full moon. If Sitting Bull were around, he'd be beside himself with envy.

Colin: As you glance at its deep, amber color, things seem to be off to a good start. Unfortunately, the malty taste doesn't deliver. No tomahawk chop for this one. 🍺🍺 ½

Randy: Native Americans may take offense at the imagery. The color is almost orange. It carries a heavy taste that shoots straight as an arrow. Dig up a little wampum and buy some. 🍺🍺🍺🍺

CHRISTIAN MOERLEIN CINCINNATI BOCK BEER

The Schoenling/Hudepohl Brewing Co.
1625 Central Pkwy.
Cincinnati, Ohio 45214
(513) 241-4344

Label Musings: A refreshing twist on the standard goat, ram or other large, horned beast that invariably graces bock beer labels. If you look closely, you'll see the ram being restrained from a glass of brew. Poor guy. Doesn't that constitute cruelty to animals?

Colin: Close your eyes while drinking this and you'll think you were sampling a stout. If that's acceptable to your palate, you may find this brew interesting. Compared to other bocks, there are a number that surpass it. I hear a Rolling Rock Bock calling my name. 🍺🍺🍺

Randy: Ring in the vernal equinox properly by drinking a good bock. You need look no further than this malty, not-too-sweet example. Beware, after having a few too many bocks you may feel compelled to butt heads with your drinking buddy. 🍺🍺🍺

CHRISTIAN MOERLEIN DOPPEL DARK

The Schoenling/Hudepohl Brewing Co.
1625 Central Parkway
Cincinnati, Ohio 45214
(513) 241-4344

Label Musings: Gold foiled neck exudes class. Black and cream label with a sketch of a beer-loving beauty from the Middle Ages.

Colin: Though its color is opaque and it seems to be a strong mixture, I found the flavor a touch on the light side. Nonetheless, it's moderately pleasing, but it won't wow you.

Randy: This Doppel has pop, as in potent. A confident, "complex" brew with an agreeable after-taste. European styling right here at home.

CHRISTIAN MOERLEIN SELECT

The Schoenling/Hudepohl Brewing Co.
1625 Central Parkway
Cincinnati, Ohio 45214
(513) 241-4344

Label Musings: Don't be fooled by the gold foil. This isn't fine champagne. The label declares it was the first American beer to meet the Reinheitsgebot, the German beer purity law of 1516.

Colin: To say this beer is mild doesn't quite say enough. Somewhere in the midst of the brewing process they forgot about a little thing called taste. It has a pale, thin color to match. Pass it by.

Randy: I am always deferential to pioneers, but they shouldn't be permitted to rest on their laurels. There is not a whole lot of flavor in this tepid concoction. Perhaps they have complied with the letter of the law, but certainly not its spirit. $^{1}/_{2}$

CIDER JACK PREMIUM DRY HARD CIDER

American Hard Cider Co.
535 Boylston Street
Boston, Massachusetts 02116
(617) 266-6035

Label Musings: Large, red apple and green lettering and bright green matching cap. Of course, it's not beer, but variety is the spice of life. We felt compelled to give it a whirl.

Colin: Spiked apple juice, but surprisingly pleasing to the palate. Not too sweet, so you won't wince. Give it a try. By the way, be forewarned, this is hard cider. It'll knock you on your butt if you're not careful. Get yourself some glazed doughnuts and enjoy. 🍺🍺🍺 $1/2$

Randy: This one just misses the mark. No, there's no worm in the apple, but its sweetness is marred by a bitter aftertaste. Hint: half cider, half lager makes a tasty combo called a Snakebite. 🍺🍺

COLD SPRING EXPORT

Cold Spring Brewing Co.
P.O. Box 476
Cold Spring, Minnesota 56320
(612) 685-8686

Label Musings: Wild, busy label on beige background. The disjointed lettering makes it look like a ransom note. Neat white and blue cap.

Colin: For a beer that touts its use of "bubbly" cold spring water, I found it surprisingly a little flat with a muted, nonthreatening taste. Turn a cold shoulder to this one. 🍺🍺

Randy: Bland and mild. Just where do they export this stuff? No wonder the trade deficit is through the roof. Corn used in the brewing process is considered by some to be a cheap extender. You can detect a hint of it in the aftertaste. I can't say it makes the brew better. 🍺🍺

COLD SPRING SELECT STOCK

Cold Spring Brewing Co.
P.O. Box 476
Cold Spring, Minnesota 56320
(612) 685-8686

Label Musings: Golden label proudly proclaims that this is a select stock from a brewery that's been doing its thing since 1874.

Colin: Many brewers are prone to bragging about the "special" water they use in their beer. In this case, the boasts are warranted. A clear, crisp flavor and tenacious finish. It earns its "select" label. 🍺🍺🍺 ½

Randy: Tart, golden brew. A winner from a brewery that is older than the Statue of Liberty. Who needs imports? Oh, and yes, it also goes great with pizza.
🍺🍺🍺 ½

CRAZY ED'S BLACK MOUNTAIN GOLD

Black Mountain Brewing Co., Inc.
P.O. Box 1940
Cave Creek, Arizona 85331
(800) 228-9742

Label Musings: Simple black and gold with a desert scene and a hot red sun setting behind a cactus.

Colin: On a boiling day in the Mohave, you'll appreciate this smooth, light brew. It is amazingly refreshing. Ed's not crazy; he knows exactly what he's doing. 🍺🍺🍺🍺 ½

Randy: After sampling that wacky chili stuff pro- duced by Ed (Ed's Chili Beer), this crisp, pale, golden beer nearly knocked me out of my seat. I could drink it all day, check, all week. Of course, I'll be ham- mered. Keep those chili peppers on your nachos.
🍺🍺🍺🍺🍺

DEMPSEY'S ALE

Joseph Huber Brewing Company, Inc.
P.O. Box 277
1208 14th Avenue
Monroe, Wisconsin 53566
(608) 325-3191

Label Musings: The word "Slainte" is prominent. Beats us what it means. Neither can we make heads or tails of the building and ship pictured. The label is red and the bottle is green; that much we're sure of.

Colin: It's unmistakably an ale. Bold and brazen. Recommended for serious beer drinkers who don't mind a powerful brew. Stick with it and you may come to swear by it. It's a knockout. 🍺🍺🍺🍺

Randy: Packs a punch like most ales brewed in the Irish style. It's certainly worthy enough to bear the name of the hard-hitting pugilist. Palatable and distinctive, I suggest you sample Mr. Dempsey's handiwork. 🍺🍺🍺 1/2

DESCHUTES JUBELALE

Deschutes Brewery, Inc.
1044 N.W. Bond Street
Bend, Oregon 97701
(503) 382-9242

Label Musings: Cartoonish wreath with funky mountain valley and peak. Very slick.

Colin: Just short of eggnog in viscosity and only a tad less creamy. Try it only when you're in the most festive of moods. 🍺🍺

Randy: A cacophony of flavor. Brackish, bitter, spicy and tangy. Perhaps too much for one glass. Maybe it goes well with rich foods, but it may overwhelm you on its own. I'm less than jubilant over this one. 🍺🍺

DIXIE

Dixie Brewing Company, Inc.
2537 Tulane Avenue
New Orleans, Louisiana 70119
(504) 822-8711

Label Musings: The straightforward label proclaims
"DIXIE." There are no stars and bars, but the crest
looks like it's suited for a battle flag. It bespeaks a
certain regional prestige.

Colin: In one word: smooth. It goes down easily,
like silk, or in deference to our friends from the South,
like combed cotton. The mild, mellow taste captures
the spirit of the Big Easy.

Randy: Abounds with husky, woody flavor. If you're
at Mardi Gras or in town for the Sugar Bowl, and are
tired of Hurricanes, you should try it. I liked it. It's a
real Southern charmer.

DIXIE BLACKENED VOODOO LAGER

Dixie Brewing Company, Inc.
2537 Tulane Avenue
New Orleans, Louisiana 70119
(504) 822-8711

Label Musings: This beer may be seeking to become
the official beer of the occult with its ominous and
sinister swamp scene. Maybe Stephen King has taken
up microbrewing. We think we see a bat in the
cypress tree.

Colin: Its name certainly fits. I don't know what's in
this potion, but I didn't fall under its spell. Watery,
tepid brew isn't frightening, just lifeless. I may grab a
six-pack on Halloween.

Randy: It is dark, like stout, but it is a lager. It seems
to have a swamp water quality. You should try one
and then tell all your friends you had a Voodoo. Then
forget about this one-trick pony. Voodoo? Voodon't!

DIXIE JAZZ AMBER LIGHT

Dixie Brewing Company, Inc.
2537 Tulane Avenue
New Orleans, Louisiana 70119
(504) 822-8711

Label Musings: You'll love this Big Easy spectacle. Jazzman blowing his horn and garish letters blaring out "JAZZ" complement this fun label. Where's the party?

Colin: Could use a fair amount of jazzin' up. They should have put the emphasis on the amber rather than the light. Pleasant enough flavor, but it won't get the joint jumping. 🍺 1/2

Randy: Only 92 calories. Why do microbreweries insist on foisting light ambers and ales upon us? These beers are meant to be full and rich. This one is tepid and watery. It doesn't make beautiful music; it just strikes sour chords. 🍺

DOCK STREET AMBER BEER

Dock Street Brewing Co.
Two Logan Square
18th and Cherry Streets
Philadelphia, Pennsylvania 19103
(215) 496-0413

Label Musings: The wayward seaman depicted lounging on a huge anchor, looks like he's been away at sea too long. Love those bell-bottoms.

Colin: W.C. Fields always said that he'd rather be in Philadelphia, and so will you after sampling this beer. There's plenty of flavor, yet it's not overwhelming. This potent amber ale would be perfect during a Phillies game at the Vet. 🍺🍺🍺🍺

Randy: From the potent, hoppy flavor you can tell that this is an upscale beer. Yet, I could even see Lenny Dykstra drinking this stuff. A Philly cheesesteak and a couple of these and you've got yourself a gourmet meal. 🍺🍺🍺🍺

DOCK STREET BOHEMIAN PILSNER BEER

Dock Street Brewing Co.
Two Logan Square
18th and Cherry Streets
Philadelphia, Pennsylvania 19103
(215) 496-0413

Label Musings: A lovely siren in a sailor outfit with a plunging neckline. You know, there aren't enough women gracing beer labels. Gee, we sound like feminists. Actually, she's a doll.

Colin: It fancies itself a "voluptuous" pilsner beer, and you'll agree after catching a glimpse of that comely lass on the label. Surprisingly, this vixen provides quite a bit of bite. 🍺🍺🍺

Randy: Throw your arms around this luscious brew. Delicate, yet malty. I'm staying home with this brew Saturday night. That's really sad. 🍺🍺🍺 ½

DOMINION ALE

Old Dominion Brewing Co.
44633 Guilford Drive
Ashburn, Virginia 22011
(703) 689-1225

Label Musings: Amber silhouetted buck over brown and purple background. He's looking for something. A nice, salty pretzel, perhaps?

Colin: The Commonwealth of Virginia now has an official ale, but it doesn't quite measure up to other offerings from around the country. No breakthrough here. Maybe it would taste better with venison. 🍺🍺

Randy: That deer is one bitter beast and he bites, too. Tolerable, but indistinguishable from other mediocre brands. Remember, there are a bunch of wonderful ales on the market. This is no standout. 🍺

DOMINION LAGER

Old Dominion Brewing Co.
44633 Guilford Drive
Ashburn, Virginia 22011
(703) 689-1225

Label Musings: Deer on busy label. The bottling date on the side is a nice touch. It's always good to know that the brew is fresh.

Colin: Virginia is for lovers, and now it's for beer drinkers also. There's a refreshing taste and crispness that'll perk you up after a long day. Call a drinking buddy and kill a six. 🍺🍺🍺

Randy: Agreeable flavor and light enough for more than one. Slightly bitter aftertaste, but very competently done. The South has risen again. Robert E. Lee would be proud. 🍺🍺🍺

DOMINION STOUT

Old Dominion Brewing Co.
44633 Guilford Drive
Ashburn, Virginia 22011
(703) 689-1225

Label Musings: That's one big buck! Silhouetted deer centrally framed by wheat and flashy lettering.

Colin: It seems Dominion is launching a new variety of beer under the guise of a stout; black coffee in a bottle. I know the espresso craze rivals the micro phenomenon in popularity, but this is ridiculous. Whether or not it's the intention of the brewers, that java flavor comes through loud and clear. What's next, decaf and French roast? 🍺🍺

Randy: Chocolaty, smooth and malty, it almost doesn't taste like beer. One of the sweeter stouts. Weaker head than most, but creamy. Although many would think otherwise, most stouts have low alcohol content (less than 5%). Don't be intimidated, give it a try. C'mon, live a little. 🍺🍺🍺

ED'S ORIGINAL CAVE CREEK CHILI BEER

Black Mountain Brewing Co., Inc.
P.O. Box 1940
Cave Creek, Arizona 85331
(800) 228-9742

Label Musings: Its tranquil pastels are deceiving. You'll find a serrano chili pepper floating in the long neck stem of each bottle. This ingenious approach is surely a conversation starter and it's bound to get national attention.

Colin: Where's the fire? It's in the bottle! If you love four-alarm chili or are bent on self-destruction, give it a shot. It's a scorcher. It was actually quite appealing to me beyond the novelty. However, I can't imagine drinking more than one. Then again, it's your funeral. 🍺🍺🍺 ½

Randy: Beer isn't supposed to hurt. There may be a market for crazed masochists, but I've got my own problems. The standard warning label says some stuff about driving and pregnant women; it really should warn the entire beer-drinking population about this particular brew. Challenge your friends' masculinity in a chugging contest. I added a "bottlecap" for exceptional creativity. 🍺🍺🍺

ELM CITY CONNECTICUT ALE

The New Haven Brewing Company
458 Grand Avenue
New Haven, Connecticut 06513
(203) 772-2739

Label Musings: We are frustrated because we don't understand what "Elm City" means. There is a picture of a columned building that's worthy of Athens, Rome or Washington, D.C. Is it the Beer Capitol?

Colin: A commendable beer that's right on the fundamentals. Not a trendsetter, but it has a pleasant taste and a clean, crisp finish. Perhaps a little on the light side. 🍺🍺🍺

Randy: There is a hint of cherry flavor with no aftertaste. These guys from Yale's hometown should encourage that university to teach a class in brewing. I would demand a scholarship. Finally, an Ivy League degree that's worth something. 🍺🍺🍺

EMERALD CITY ALE

Emerald City Brewing Co.
3100 Airport Way South
Seattle, Washington 98134
(206) 292-9677

Label Musings: Emerald label with art deco sketch of Seattle's ever-growing skyline. With slogan, "Where it reigns, it pours." We caught Joel Fleischman throwing one back on Northern Exposure.

Colin: The brewmaster responsible for cooking up this beer is a wizard indeed. As long as it is available at the nearest saloon, I may not want to go home again. Auntie Em was no prize anyway. A skillfully-brewed, fresh ale that is just delicious. 🍺🍺🍺🍺 ½

Randy: The wet and wonderful Emerald City of Seattle is home to many fine microbreweries like this one. A sip of this brew and you'll know what I mean. For some time, the Pacific Northwest has led the industry in great beers produced by small, local breweries. Keep it up, there's room for more. Too bad it rains so much. 🍺🍺🍺🍺

EYE OF THE HAWK

Mendocino Brewing Co.
P.O. Box 400
Hopland, California 95449
(707) 744-1015

Label Musings: In a 25.4-ounce bottle, it looks like they're hawking wine. Don't be fooled, the bottle cap is a dead giveaway. A patriotic red, white and blue label with an intense hawk is a guaranteed eye-catcher.

Colin: It certainly is different, but its lackluster flavor is far from spectacular. More evidence that a great name and a great label do not always add up to a great brew. No hawk; just a turkey. 🍺🍺

Randy: All the earmarks of a special beer, but it doesn't deliver the goods. The brew is strong, yet pleasant, but it's by no means as majestic as the label. Consider bringing a bottle to a dinner party to intrigue your hosts. 🍺🍺 ½

FAMOUS OLD WEST AMBER LAGER

Old West Brewing Co.
Florida Beer Brands
New Ulm, Minnesota 56073
(800) 741-WEST

Label Musings: The guys at Old West are preserving two fixtures of our heritage: beer and gunmen. God bless 'em! Various figures from the Wild West days grace the witty labels. Among them, Bill Longley, Judge Roy Bean and the Sundance Kid. Serious collectors may want to round up the whole lot.

Colin: If you think you're tough enough, take on this take-no-prisoners brew that goes down like sandpaper. Seems that it's brewed only for those who have a frontier spirit. It has an authenticity about it that makes you take notice. Beer may be just what the West was won for. 🍺🍺🍺

Randy: Starts out sweet, ends bitter; like many westerns I've seen. No wonder the West was so wild. Brews like this give me an itchy trigger finger. See you at high noon—at the saloon. 🍺🍺 ½

FAT TIRE AMBER ALE

New Belgium Brewing Company, Inc.
350 Linden Street
Fort Collins, Colorado 80524
(303) 221-0524

Label Musings: Big, old bicycle will remind you of your first one as a kid. Strange name for a brew though.

Colin: It had a blowout. Overly sweet and not too much else. A dubious taste to match the label and the name. Maybe they should have put a dirt bike on the label, because this brew doesn't travel the straight and narrow. 🍺

Randy: Flat tire is more like it. The live yeast in the bottle adds some fullness, but it's too redolent and nutty. This beer needs training wheels. 🍺🍺

FLAGSHIP RED ALE

Maritime Pacific Brewing Co.
1514 Northwest Leary Way
Seattle, Washington 98107
(206) 782-6181

Label Musings: Good ol' clipper ship as per usual. This time the U.S.S. Brewski sails under a red banner past golden mountains.

Colin: Offers a mainstream ale taste, but is perhaps just a touch sweeter than most. Familiar enough stuff, but not the pride of the fleet. 🍺🍺

Randy: Rust-colored with a mild, lackluster flavor and acrid aftertaste. No points for creativity, but it is a solid effort. Not just for old salts. 🍺🍺

FLYING ACES LIGHT

Flying Aces Brewing Co.
Florida Beer Brands
New Ulm, Minnesota 56073
(800) 749-ACES

Label Musings: Available for purchase in the bomber bottle (22 ounces). Some labels are graced with various depictions of WWII-era fighter planes and bombers. Others have the plane-side paintings of gals the pilots left behind. Nostalgia freaks will love this one.

Colin: Proclaims itself to have a "taste above the rest." Perhaps because it tastes lighter than air. Of course, for light beer aficionados (does there exist such an animal?), it may provide some enjoyment. Otherwise, take the nonstop right by it. 🍺🍺

Randy: I'm as patriotic as they come, but I venture to guess that this tepid brew wouldn't satisfy our fighting men (and women). This is so ethereal I thought it was going to start flying around the room by itself. As far as I'm concerned, it should be grounded. 🍺

FRANKENMUTH BOCK

Frankenmuth Brewery, Inc.
425 South Main Street
Frankenmuth, Michigan 48734
(517) 652-6183

Label Musings: Frankenmuth label scheme is understated and elegant in green, red and silver.

Colin: Oh, it's a bock alright: brown, sweet and brawny. Unabashed taste, but uncharacteristically smooth and even. Bock or not, this brew is no goat. 🍺🍺🍺 ½

Randy: This bock is quite dark, with a considerable head and lots of caramel flavor. It's one of the heartiest bocks I sampled. If you have the opportunity, attend a blessing of the bock at your local brewery. It's usually held on the first day of spring and you're sure to have a blast. 🍺🍺🍺🍺

FRANKENMUTH DARK

Frankenmuth Brewery, Inc.
425 South Main Street
Frankenmuth, Michigan 48734
(517) 652-6183

Label Musings: Standard, simple Frankenmuth label in black, red and gold. Very sharp, but how about some originality?

Colin: Black gold. This brew will test your mettle. Dark, rich and very satisfying. My compliments to Dr. Frankenmuth; he's created a monster of a beer. 🍺🍺🍺🍺

Randy: Roasted over an open fire. Although they don't say as much, this tastes like a porter. It has that characteristic burnt flavor, dark color, even taste and light fluidity. It's a solid porter. 🍺🍺🍺 ½

FRANKENMUTH EXTRA LIGHT

Frankenmuth Brewery, Inc.
425 South Main Street
Frankenmuth, Michigan 48734
(517) 652-6183

Label Musings: Snazzy green, silver and white on a green bottle. Certainly stands out. It's got nutritional info on the label. Beer is a health food? Gee, now all of us beer drinkers can look forward to long, happy lives.

Colin: Extra light is right. I'd love to offer you my opinion, but I can't recall any flavor. What taste is present is decidedly sour. In other words, a very forgettable beer. Water out of the tap will easily provide just as much excitement. 🍺

Randy: It's only 97 calories. Admittedly, it's tough to make a flavorful light, but this is an especially weak effort. Sometimes the joy of drinking a "real" beer is worth an extra lap tomorrow. 🍺

FRANKENMUTH PILSNER

Frankenmuth Brewery, Inc.
425 South Main Street
Frankenmuth, Michigan 48734
(517) 652-6183

Label Musings: Standard Frankenmuth label, this time in red, silver and navy. Although there seems to be a number of ways to spell it, they chose the way we prefer: P-I-L-S-N-E-R.

Colin: Clean, clear and crisp. A very solid pilsner, if not extraordinary. One of these will refresh you on a hot summer day. Well handled and very enjoyable.
🍺🍺🍺 ¹/₂

Randy: Quite light, in both color and taste. You can see clear to the bottom of your mug. This beer would be ideal for playing "Quarters." You'll see that coin sink all the way down. 🍺🍺

FRANKENMUTH WEISSE

Frankenmuth Brewery, Inc.
425 South Main Street
Frankenmuth, Michigan 48734
(517) 652-6183

Label Musings: Aqua on white with the standard Frankenmuth label scheme.

Colin: Mild, crisp and remarkably refreshing. This beer should be your just reward after yard work, an outing at the gym or a long day on the job. Absolutely delicious. 🍺🍺🍺🍺🍺

Randy: Hefeweizen—that is, wheat beer brewed with yeast. Roll the bottle in your hands before you pour. Then let it rip. It has a bountiful head and a perfectly cloudy color, just as it should be. So much wheat flavor that you'll feel like you've been transported to Bavaria. 🍺🍺🍺🍺🍺

FULL SAIL AMBER ALE

Full Sail Brewing Co.
506 Columbia Street
Hood River, Oregon 97031
(503) 386-2281

Label Musings: Unfurled, orange sail on a boat ambling downriver. Earned a gold medal at the Great American Beer Festival. Maybe it's due to their use of Mount Hood spring water.

Colin: This beer's name says it all. Nothing has been held back in this full-flavored ale. But don't worry, it has a very smooth finish to boot. Remember, it's an ale, so break it out only when you've dropped anchor for the night. 🍺🍺🍺🍺

Randy: Powerful ale with burnt, hearty flavor. Just a little uneven and unwieldy. It's for you if you want to open her up full throttle, batten down the hatches and hoist the mizzenmast. 🍺🍺🍺

FULL SAIL GOLDEN ALE

Full Sail Brewing Co.
506 Columbia Street
Hood River, Oregon 97031
(503) 386-2281

Label Musings: Golden, open sail backed by blue mountain scenery and rapids. A snowcapped peak in the background finishes off the look. Gotta love those nature scenes.

Colin: A superior beer. I give it high marks across the board. With a light, urbane palate, it's a pleasure to imbibe. Stock up on this one and throw your own Operation Sail. 🍺🍺🍺🍺🍺

Randy: Ah, the thought of sailing along a mountain lake on a sunny summer's day with a picnic basket, some friends and a cooler stocked with this crisp, palatable and refreshing golden ale. It would be heaven on earth. Or at least the makings of a good beer commercial. 🍺🍺🍺🍺 ¹/₂

GATOR LIGHT LAGER BEER

Florida Beer Brands
645 W. Michigan Street
Orlando, Florida 32805
(407) 423-3929

Label Musings: There's nothing light about that massive gator staring at you. He looks as if he'd swallow you whole in nothing flat. The eagle that shares the label must be scrambling to take flight in a hurry. We've noticed that Florida Beer Brands produces quite creative labels.

Colin: This beer has no teeth. A toothless alligator? This is microbrewed beer and as such it should adhere to certain standards. Forget it. Don't buy it for the picture. If you've got a hankering for a light beer, you might as well bite the silver bullet. 🍺

Randy: Why in the name of heaven would you brew a light beer and use a ferocious alligator as your spokes-animal? So much for gimmicks. Another lame attempt at winning over guilt-ridden weight watchers. 🍺

GEARY'S HAMPSHIRE SPECIAL WINTER ALE

**D.L. Geary Brewing Co.
38 Evergreen Drive
Portland, Maine 04103
(207) 878-2337**

Label Musings: Quaint, small, wintery town on a granite background. It's almost too pretty for a beer label.

Colin: I think the fellas at Geary's have gotten a little too fancy here. The aftertaste is overwhelming. If you drink too much of this stuff, you'll be tasting it for days. 🍺 ½

Randy: It is a sumptuous, dark and malty ale. Serve it cold and it will keep you toasty warm. Serve it warm and those spices will surface. Almost as if it were art as beer. 🍺🍺🍺 ½

GEARY'S PALE ALE

**D.L. Geary Brewing Co.
38 Evergreen Drive
Portland, Maine 04103
(207) 878-2337**

Label Musings: Perhaps one of the best labels on the micro scene. State pride is reflected in a three-pound lobster on a black background and the letter "G" over a map of Maine.

Colin: Since I'm not dining on lobster thermidor nightly, I may not be fit to review this beer. It's so bitter and potent it makes me a little woozy. Tasty, but may not fit into the mainstream. That's OK, we'll keep it our little secret. 🍺🍺 ½

Randy: Extremely potent for a pale ale. It's hard to overcome a bitter flavor and chemistry-set odor. Is this what they drink up in Kennebunkport? Perhaps this concoction may have clouded Mr. Bush's judgment and cost him his job. I'd rather eat that lobster with a lot of melted butter. 🍺🍺

GENESEE 12 HORSE ALE

The Genesee Brewing Co., Inc.
445 St. Paul Street
Rochester, New York 14605
(716) 546-1030

Label Musings: Green bottle. Classy team of Clydesdales coming at you. The folks in St. Louis shouldn't be jealous. Imitation is the sincerest form of flattery.

Colin: Strictly standard. This beer needs more horsepower. Genesee has stuck with a proven method and more power to them. But it is not worth a detour from your standby brew. 🍺🍺

Randy: Not a heck of a lot of flavor. Genesee is a fairly large brewery, but it may not be well known outside the Northeast. This beer isn't worth spreading the word. 🍺🍺

GENESEE CREAM ALE

The Genesee Brewing Co., Inc.
445 St. Paul Street
Rochester, New York 14605
(716) 546-1030

Label Musings: Nothing much to say about this small green and gold label. A label that speaks softly from a brewery that carries a big stick.

Colin: Creamy, sweet and delicious. If you steer clear of ale because it's too strong for your tastes, this one is your pick. Nice and smooth. Go grab a Genny. 🍺🍺🍺 ¹/₂

Randy: There's a mystique about Genesee: college kids, especially lacrosse and rugby fans, bombed and swaying to Springsteen's music. As a beer "critic," I find it really light and slightly bitter. But, ah, the memories. 🍺🍺 ¹/₂

GOLDFINCH NEW JERSEY AMBER

Goldfinch Brewing Company
308 Ralston Drive
Mt. Laurel, New Jersey 08054
(609) 273-9583

Label Musings: The New Jersey state bird is in full flight on this extremely colorful label with a yellow and black goldfinch that would make Mr. Audubon proud. Also, the green bottle with gold cap is terrific.

Colin: Enigmatic, murky and unpalatable. As a New Jersey native, I'd love to shout praises for this home-grown beer, but the taste isn't clean or crisp enough for me. 🍺🍺

Randy: Dark, pungent lager with big-time flavor. Strong aftertaste, which is to be expected from so much taste. Strikes me as similar to Samuel Adams Boston Ale. Good job for a small brewery. 🍺🍺🍺

GRANT'S APPLE HONEY ALE

Yakima Brewing & Malting Company
P.O. Box 9158
Yakima, Washington 98909-0158
(509) 575-1900

Label Musings: A bright red Washington apple graces the label as Farmer Grant speaks to us from the apple orchard to push another of his innovative recipes. He explains that pure apple juice and the finest Northwest honey are used in the brewing process.

Colin: Given its billing, I was expecting (and looking forward to) a sweet, pleasant tasting beer. Instead, I found a rather sour and disagreeable mixture. When out picking beers, make a beeline for one of Mr. Grant's more enticing offerings. 🍺 1/2

Randy: What's next? Blueberry bran? I say keep the fruit and honey in cereal and muffins. Farmer Grant should stick to growing hops and let the government pay him not to harvest apples. What did I like about this beer? Nut'n'honey. 🍺

GRANT'S CELTIC ALE

Yakima Brewing & Malting Company
P.O. Box 9158
Yakima, Washington 98909-0158
(509) 575-1900

Label Musings: The indomitable Professor Bert Grant stands at the blackboard. His philosophy employs a twisted logic to reach its conclusion that "The greatness of the world depends on ale. And Celtic Ale is one of the world's greatest ales. And only I make it." Is Professor Grant bent on world domination? In any event, the medieval cross is a nice touch.

Colin: While I don't always see eye to eye with Mr. Grant, he's hit pay dirt with this one. This beer has made my "always in the fridge" list—a select group indeed. 🍺🍺🍺🍺

Randy: This dark and mild ale is only 99 calories? Are you sure, Prof. Grant? You don't need to drink this for any reason other than the taste; it's terrific. As I have been otherwise despondent over the lack of tasty light microbrews, this is truly an achievement. 🍺🍺🍺🍺 1/2

GRANT'S IMPERIAL STOUT

Yakima Brewing & Malting Company
P.O. Box 9158
Yakima, Washington 98909-0158
(509) 575-1900

Label Musings: Dr. Boris Grant keeps staring at you like an old curmudgeon in tweed. The Kremlin on the label is an interesting touch, but we don't get it. Didn't we win the Cold War? Actually, Imperial Stout is a classic beer style.

Colin: While the Russians have had their problems, nobody ever doubted their fondness for a good drink. For certain, this isn't for everyone, but for those who are nostalgic for the days of the Evil Empire, it does have a certain appeal. Even Ronald Reagan would approve. 🍺🍺🍺 1/2

Randy: It stained my mug! Chocolate color, overpowering hop flavor and a bitter aftertaste. The label states that this brew was a favorite of the Russian Czar. Well, look what happened to him. Stick to espresso if you need a jolt. 🍺 1/2

GRANT'S INDIA PALE ALE

Yakima Brewing & Malting Company
P.O. Box 9158
Yakima, Washington 98909-0158
(509) 575-1900

Label Musings: On this colorful label, the Taj Mahal jumps at you as two guards, one British, one Indian, guard the tomb and the brew. The smirking Captain Bert Grant stands by as the last line of defense.

Colin: This beer is certainly unique. Perhaps it has tried too hard to become so. Why did the British make this beer for export? Maybe because they wanted to get it out of the country. 🍺 ½

Randy: This ale has an impressive, distinct flavor. Hardly relevant to its taste, but it's paler than most pale ales. Would Gandhi have led a revolution if he had been drinking this mellifluous brew? 🍺🍺🍺 ½

GRANT'S SCOTTISH ALE

Yakima Brewing & Malting Company
P.O. Box 9158
Yakima, Washington 98909-0158
(509) 575-1900

Label Musings: Most Reverend MacGrant isn't wearing his tartan kilt. From his exalted pulpit at the brewery he speaks to us in dramatic tones, "There's good ale. There's great ale. And then there's my Scottish Ale . . . I think this is the world's best ale."

Colin: Mr. Grant has a lot to brag about with this one. This magnificent achievement in brewing is not only bursting with flavor, but goes down nice and easy. I detect a hint of butterscotch. Is that your secret, Mr. Grant? You will truly be cheating yourself if you don't track this one down. After this magical brew takes effect, you may feel compelled to wear a kilt around the house. 🍺🍺🍺🍺🍺

Randy: When you boast like Rev. MacGrant, you'd better back it up with more than just the good book. The world's best ale? It just may be. It delivers perhaps the most delectable beer flavor I've had the pleasure of sampling. Rev. MacGrant is certain to round up plenty of converts with this one. 🍺🍺🍺🍺🍺

GRANT'S SPICED ALE

Yakima Brewing & Malting Company
P.O. Box 9158
Yakima, Washington 98909-0158
(509) 575-1900

Label Musings: That merry chap, Ol' St. Grant brings us his "mulled" ale. From his lofty perch atop the label he boasts with pride, "this product [is] the first of its kind in bottles anywhere in the world." What a salesman.

Colin: Like all of Grant's offerings, this one has distinctive qualities. Remember, this is spiced ale and shouldn't be guzzled out of a frosty mug. Instead, it should be served warm and maybe even with a cinnamon stick if you like. A nice change of pace to ward off a chill on cold winter nights. 🍺🍺🍺🍺

Randy: Well, it has lots of spicy goodness. This could easily be called a winter or Christmas ale. Ol' St. Grant does it again. Cozy up to an open fire and enjoy. Just remember to douse the flames on Christmas Eve or Santa is gonna get pissed. 🍺🍺🍺🍺

GRANT'S WEIS BEER

Yakima Brewing & Malting Company
P.O. Box 9158
Yakima, Washington 98909-0158
(509) 575-1900

Label Musings: Look for the big white bear. "Weis beer" means wheat beer. Brewing with wheat is a German concept, but one that is gaining increasing popularity in the States. This label has a lumbering polar bear skulking around the Arctic. Of course, Kaiser von Grant strikes a pose.

Colin: Verrry interesting. Look, I'm no farm boy, but this brings on a strange compulsion to bale hay. It's a beer you just can't help gulping. The future of beer may well be paved with fields of wheat. 🍺🍺🍺🍺

Randy: When I was in Bavaria last year, I was downing wheat beer like it was going out of style because there ain't much to be found in America. Well, I expect it to be in style in the U.S.A. very soon. It's about thirty percent malted wheat. This one has an uncommon, fruity, potent taste. Get a big frosted glass and some weisswurst (white, spring Bavarian sausage) and have a blast. 🍺🍺🍺🍺 ¹/₂

GROWLIN' GATOR LAGER

Florida Beer Brands
645 W. Michigan Street
Orlando, Florida 32805
(407) 423-3929

Label Musings: Cartoonish, sunglass-wearing gator dude partying amid Florida's famous palms. Proclaims itself the "Favorite of Lounge Lizards Everywhere." Alligator as beer pitch man? That huckster, cigarette-smoking camel better look out.

Colin: Seems as though this gator's been defanged. Mild to the point of blandness, this brew is no standout. Of course, if you're planning a Florida beach party, this would be a fitting choice. You know, when in Rome. 🍺🍺

Randy: Slogans galore: "The beer with a bite," "Enjoy a taste of Florida lifestyle," "European flavor without the bitterness." Lots of slogans, no flavor. I'd wrestle that toothless, gummy gator anytime. 🍺 ½

HARPOON ALE

Mass. Bay Brewing Co., Inc.
306 Northern Avenue
Boston, Massachusetts 02210
(617) 574-9551

Label Musings: They've silhouetted the harpoonist over a yellow background to make him look less imposing, but don't delude yourself, he's still on the hunt. There is another version on the market with a picture of the harpoonist. Perhaps the brewery fears the wrath of the politically correct "save the whales" crowd. We don't think they drink much beer anyway.

Colin: Strictly for the crew of the Pequod. Hearty and bitter, it seems to have been brewed with rough and tumble seafarers and their landlubber soul mates in mind. Not a whale of an ale by any means. 🍺🍺

Randy: This ale has a balanced finish and is blended nicely. But it's a little bitter. Overall, not a direct hit, but quite drinkable. Take a full cooler on your next fishing trip. 🍺🍺🍺

HARPOON GOLDEN LAGER

Mass. Bay Brewing Co., Inc.
306 Northern Avenue
Boston, Massachusetts 02210
(607) 574-9551

Label Musings: A colorful and artistic mix of yellow, green and white. The label states it's "fresh, without the 'skunkiness' found in beers that travel great distances in green bottles." Because we are not among that breed apart that prefers "skunky" beer, that tidbit of information was most welcome.

Colin: Don't be misled, this brew tastes more like an ale than a lager. Whatever its identity, the result is not particularly noteworthy. Some brewers which offer many varieties should consider sticking to the worthiest ones. Remember, it's quality not quantity that has generated the microbrew revolution. Stray from that credo, and the mystique is out the window.

Randy: Strangely, the hoppy flavor is there, albeit bitter, but this potion doesn't overwhelm you with taste. This lifeless brew needs a little more backbone. Cloudy brew may need to be filtered through some baleen. To its credit, the label is right: no skunkiness. 🍺 ¹/₂

HARPOON LIGHT

Mass. Bay Brewing Co., Inc.
306 Northern Avenue
Boston, Massachusetts 02210
(617) 574-9551

Label Musings: Missing that picture of the harpoonist armed to the hilt. That's the brewery's name, stick to the theme. Quoteth the label, "Harpoon Light is brewed specifically to be a light beer, not a watered down version of the regular beer." Dizzying, abstract geometric design.

Colin: One of the great aspects of the micro craze is the availability of a few, truly great tasting offerings in the light beer category. Harpoon Light is a perfect example. Without its moniker, you would never know it's a light. 🍺🍺🍺🍺

Randy: Now we're talking. Here's an excellent light beer that is comparable to the flavor of other regular beers at half the calories. Wonderful, now I can drink twice as much. 🍺🍺🍺🍺

HARPOON OCTOBERFEST

Mass. Bay Brewing Co., Inc.
306 Northern Ave.
Boston, Massachusetts 02210
(617) 574-9551

Label Musings: You're invited to the Harpoon Octoberfest at the brewery in Boston. The label suggests you call (617) 455-1935 for info. The colorful leaves on the label are a reminder that October is a sacred month for beer lovers.

Colin: Ah, autumn. The bright foliage, football games and those great Octoberfest beers. While a robust member of the class, this beer also comes equipped with plenty of drinkability. After a backbreaking session of raking leaves in the yard, treat yourself to a few. 🍺🍺🍺 ½

Randy: This sour ale has distinctive flavor. Maybe you'll fall for it once a year. Still, it's got character and once the heat breaks, I'll give it another go in the fridge. It won't give you a "Nantucket sleigh ride" if that's what you're after. 🍺🍺

HARPOON STOUT

Mass. Bay Brewing Co., Inc.
306 Northern Avenue
Boston, Massachusetts 02210
(617) 574-9551

Label Musings: Dark green with a sketch of hops. The neck label states that head brewer Tod Mott uses six kinds of two row malt. Signature red "H" in white diamond on cap.

Colin: Robust with a molasses nose, but fails on the follow through. The sour aftertaste slightly detracts from the overall effect. If you're a stout fanatic, you may want to sample it. Otherwise, stay out of range of this harpoon. 🍺🍺

Randy: Heavy, so you may have to come up for air. Smooth and creamy with a licorice finish, this fine stout would go splendidly with a rare filet mignon. Is it dinner time yet? 🍺🍺🍺

HARPOON WINTER WARMER

Mass. Bay Brewing Co., Inc.
306 Northern Avenue
Boston, Massachusetts 02210
(617) 574-9551

Label Musings: Festive, seasonal label. Santa may know if you've been bad or good, but he doesn't know beer (he's a Scotch drinker from way back). Leave the beer verdicts to us.

Colin: Scratch spiked eggnog off your holiday cheer lineup. Stock up on this festive mix of quality beer and zesty spices. It will put you in an upbeat mood all year long. 🍺🍺🍺🍺 ½

Randy: The addition of cinnamon and nutmeg made my cheeks rosy. This is a bracing, spicy ale. In the spirit of the season, a six-pack would be a great li'l something under the tree for all us overgrown kids. 🍺🍺🍺🍺

HELENBOCH BEER

Friends Brewing Company
P.O. Box 29464
Atlanta, Georgia 30359
(404) 986-8505

Label Musings: Modern art-inspired drawing of a huge "H" over a church's steeple. Stately and elegant.

Colin: This Munich Helles-style beer has a racy, complex flavor, and retains a remarkably smooth consistency to boot. You'll love its deep amber color. Despite its full-bodied taste, it doesn't wear you down. Quite an accomplishment indeed. 🍺🍺🍺🍺 ½

Randy: There is a ton of luxuriant, smooth, even flavor. It could be an international smash if these Atlanta brewers get visitors to the 1996 Summer Olympics hooked. Strikingly simple label that seems to have been inspired by the Quakers (Friends). I believe I've made some new friends. 🍺🍺🍺🍺 ½

HENRY WEINHARD'S PRIVATE RESERVE

Blitz-Weinhard Co.
1133 West Burnside Street
Portland, Oregon 97209
(503) 222-4351

Label Musings: You'll hardly believe that it's a domestic with the stately gold and beige label with eagle in a crest. Informs us that "thirty-seven individual brewing steps assure absolute quality." Gee, would all be lost if they left out step number 28?

Colin: This stuff is almost indistinguishable from the big name brands. It does have a crisp, clean quality. Nifty touch putting a bottling number on; mine was number 118. Makes you feel like a member of Henry Weinhard's club. 🍺🍺🍺

Randy: Extremely pale, with a delicate bitter flavor and clean finish. If you enjoy pale pilsners, you'll feel like you're in the presence of American royalty. Thoroughly refreshing. 🍺🍺🍺🍺 ¹/₂

HOBOKEN SPECIAL RESERVE ALE

The Gold Coast Brewery
c/o The New Haven Brewing Company
458 Grand Avenue
New Haven, Connecticut 06513
(203) 772-2739

Label Musings: Shouldn't the label of a beer named after Hoboken, New Jersey have a likeness of Frank Sinatra on it? Instead, the standard clipper ship was chosen. Tres cliche.

Colin: This ale doesn't overpower you, but it is extremely tasty. If it was available in the hinterlands, it would likely create a sensation. These brewers did it their way. 🍺🍺🍺🍺

Randy: Crisp, tight pale ale with a slightly bitter aftertaste and an alcohol odor. While named for the birthplace of Francis Albert, I think Ol' Blue Eyes prefers the harder stuff. 🍺🍺🍺

HOWLIN' STOUT

Onalaska Brewing Co.
248 Burchett Road
Onalaska, Washington 98570
(206) 978-4253

Label Musings: Sharp label with black, lavender and white. You can't miss that howlin' pooch. Is he howlin' for his dinner or another brewski?

Colin: I howled when I realized this stout lacks the frothy, creamy head and finish found in more accomplished varieties. By no means is it doggone good.  ¹/₂

Randy: Honeyed, burnt flavor, but not enough of that heavy, bitter flavor stout fans crave. Sorry to say, there's no howl here, merely a whimper. ¹/₂

I.C. SELECT GOLDEN LAGER

Pittsburgh Brewing Company
3340 Liberty Avenue
Pittsburgh, Pennsylvania 15201
(412) 682-7400

Label Musings: A stocky, little, old-fashioned bottle hails from a brewery that's been cranking it out since the Civil War. Not exactly a new kid on the block.

Colin: No groundbreaker here. Weak, tepid lager that is downright uninteresting. There's much better out there, folks. ¹/₂

Randy: If this is what was selected, I'd hate to sample the batch they dumped out back. The aftertaste contains a quirky, fruity flavor. Very disappointing.

ICEHOUSE

The Plank Road Brewery
Miller Brewing Company
3939 West Highland Boulevard
Milwaukee, Wisconsin 53201
(800) 645-5376

Label Musings: If you're not one for the cold, it may not be for you. The winter scene depicted looks like it was commissioned from some hack, second-rate "artist." With all the cash invested in the advertising push by Miller, you'd think we'd see something spectacular.

Colin: I don't know what the ice-brewing fuss is all about. In the brewing process, the temperature gets low enough for ice crystals to form. So what! There is nothing unique in the taste. However, it is light, pale and refreshing, like a pilsner. 🍺🍺🍺

Randy: The Plank Road Brewery is the original name of Miller. There is a manly head and a slightly chemical nose, but not much punch. This may be one for those who don't like the taste of beer; because there isn't much flavor. Ice, dry, what's the big deal? 🍺🍺 ¹/₂

JAMAICA BRAND RED ALE

Mad River Brewing Co.
P.O. Box 767
Blue Lake, California 95525
(707) 668-4151

Label Musings: Wild, rasta yellow label with a shock of green and red stars. An explosion of color from reggae land. But, it's from California, not a Caribbean isle.

Colin: Hey, mon, if you like a little spice in your ale, give this one a try. Now, you don't need to fly to Negril to sample a Jamaican brew. Unless you're partial to topless beaches. Cool runnings to you. 🍺🍺🍺 ¹/₂

Randy: Dark, rose-colored amber ale. Mild and mellow like the island nation. Throw some Bob Marley in the CD player and drink. It'll be an instant vacation. 🍺🍺🍺 ¹/₂

JET CITY PALE ALE

Jet City Brewing Company
3125 234 Court S.E.
Issaquah, Washington 98027
(206) 392-5991

Label Musings: Zooming jet with Jetsons' space age lettering. Label extols it is "as smooth and unsurpassed as the famous 'Slow Roll' of 1955, the legendary flying feat." Of course, unless you're an aviation insider, you'll be puzzled like us.

Colin: There's a tingling sensation from the carbonation akin to ginger ale that comes through. Light, refreshing and cohesive flavor. Grab a six-pack and you'll be flying in first class. 🍺🍺🍺 ½

Randy: Zestful, tangy ale. This beer will definitely "take off." I guess Jet City is another nickname for the city of Seattle, which is the home of Boeing. This is a high-flying, slow-rolling brew. 🍺🍺🍺 ½

J.J. WAINWRIGHT'S SELECT LAGER

Pittsburgh Brewing Company
3340 Liberty Avenue
Pittsburgh, Pennsylvania 15201
(412) 682-7400

Label Musings: Script on raised glass is quite polished. Ample, informative label over superimposed sketch of a columned building.

Colin: You'll taste the malt the instant it reaches your palate. This lager has a deep amber color that's easy on the eyes, even without beer goggles. Overall, an admirable job. 🍺🍺🍺 ½

Randy: Truly malty and flavorful. It must be a favorite of Steelers' fans, as fuel to get them through a battle at Three Rivers Stadium against the Browns in December. Get with the program, get a couple of sixes. Make it a case. There's always a chance for overtime. 🍺🍺🍺🍺

JOHN BARLEYCORN BARLEYWINE STYLE ALE

Mad River Brewing Company
P.O. Box 767
Blue Lake, California 95525
(707) 668-4151

Label Musings: Medieval artwork of a corn farmer. Quoteth the label, "Then with a plow they ploughed him up, And thus they did devise, to bury him with the earth, And swore he would not rise." Certainly one of the more creative labels you'll find, whatever it means.

Colin: In my humble opinion, this beer does not warrant making it to your short list. If it's wine you want, I suggest a nice Chablis, but if it's beer you crave, barleywine ale may be a rude surprise. 🍺 1/2

Randy: Your spine will shiver after just one sip. The spicy barleywine is overwhelming. A pungent odor and a sweet palate are also evident. It'll transport you back to King Arthur's Court and remind you of the days of grog. On the other hand, it might just make you groggy. Quite original, to say the least. 🍺🍺🍺

KILLIAN'S IRISH RED

Coors Brewing Co.
Golden, Colorado 80401
(303) 279-6565

Label Musings: Distinctive, red trim around oval label. Nothing fancy. Brewed in the tradition of George Killian Lett of Enniscarthy, Ireland. His name implies that he knew what he was doing around beer.

Colin: No, it's not red, folks. Reddish, maybe. In any event, it's pretty damn good beer. The boys at Coors didn't get where they are without knowing how to put a beer together that would have mass appeal. Granted, Coors probably would just as soon stay in the background and be an inconspicuous presence on the micro shelves. Why so shy? You should be proud of your handiwork. 🍺🍺🍺🍺

Randy: Actually, this beer has been available for a while and I've been drinking it for years. Now, Coors has begun to market it as a sort of microbrew. This has a consistent sweet, caramel twang. As a capitalist, I believe it's fine for a major brewer to compete in the microbrew arena. Laissez faire, I always say. 🍺🍺🍺🍺

LANDMARK BOCK

Minnesota Brewing Co.
882 West Seventh Street
St. Paul, Minnesota 55102
(612) 228-9173

Label Musings: An original scene: a ram on some mountain. "Bock" means "ram" in German, but do they need to put one on every label? Why is this beer style so named? Is it brewed with essence of sheep?

Colin: This bock is too potent for the casual drinker. It's strictly for the hard-core bocker. It doesn't go down easily, but it's worth the effort.

Randy: It shouldn't have gotten landmark status. It's got an aftertaste that won't quit. If you're a bock fan, I think you'll find it falls short. I like the ram, though.

LEAN PIG'S EYE

Minnesota Brewing Co.
882 West Seventh Street
St. Paul, Minnesota 55102
(612) 228-9173

Label Musings: We don't think the pirate on this label would approve of light beer. Come to think of it, rum is probably his poison of choice. He wouldn't drink it out of any fine crystal glass either—right out of the cask.

Colin: Modestly appealing, light brew. If you want to go the light route, this one may provide some enjoyment. Here's mud in your eye. Pig's eye, that is.

Randy: How can you put a label with a pirate on a light beer? I believe light beer labels should have good-looking, sunglass-wearing, party-loving young people in flimsy swimsuits. Anyway, there isn't much flavor here. But you won't get fat.

LEINENKUGEL'S RED LAGER

Jacob Leinenkugel Brewing Co.
1-3 Jefferson Avenue
P.O. Box 368
Chippewa Falls, Wisconsin 54729
(715) 723-5558

Label Musings: Smart red and gold jobby with the old wooden brewery prominently displayed. Brewed since 1867, it's now owned by Miller Brewing, but under exclusive control of Jake Leinenkugel. He carries on Jacob's legend and does his ancestry proud. Maybe it's in the genes.

Colin: I've never been to Chippewa Falls, and now I know what I've been missing. One of the most even keeled and pleasant tasting beers you are likely to find anywhere. Combine the superior taste with an almost ruby red hue and creamy head, and you'll see why this veteran brewery has such a devoted following. I don't mean to badger you, but you've got to track this stuff down at all costs. You'll thank me later.

Randy: Magnificent red lager from Wisconsin way. As it slowly rolls down your gullet, you'll experience a superb malty bonanza and wonder if life can get any better. Hail Leinie's!

LIMERICK'S IRISH STYLE RED ALE

The Buffalo Brewing Company
1830 Abbott Road
Buffalo, New York 14218
(716) 828-0004

Label Musings: A label anyone who hails from the Emerald Isle would approve of. Lots of green and plenty of shamrocks. The date is March 17. Circle it on your calendar.

Colin: An extremely sour taste that simply does not subside. Not a pleasing bottle o' beer. The luck of the Irish seems to have run out.

Randy: Bitter and biting. This must be brewed by one evil leprechaun. I hope I find a pot o' gold at the end of the rainbow and not a cooler loaded with these.

LITTLE KINGS CREAM ALE

The Schoenling Brewing Co.
1625 Central Parkway
Cincinnati, Ohio 45214
(513) 241-4344

Label Musings: You can't miss the signature paw prints left by the resident bear back at the brewery. Serious fans (like us) or big drinkers (also like us) will prefer the 22-ounce bottle, but it also comes in a tiny 8-ounce size. The brewery is working with the Wilderness Society to save the Grizzly and its habitat. For info, call (800) 647-BEAR.

Colin: Too sweet for my taste. Don't let the Grizzly paw prints fool you. This brew is a teddy bear. It certainly has its strong points, but didn't quite win me over. 🍺🍺

Randy: This light ale is sweet and easy going down. Not big or bearish by any means. After 22 ounces, you'll want to hibernate. Maybe that's why it's available in little bottles. 🍺🍺🍺

LONE STAR

G. Heileman Brewing Co.
600 Lone Star Boulevard
San Antonio, Texas 78204
(210) 226-8301

Label Musings: Red lettering over silver pinstripe and big gold star. They sure promote the use of Artesian spring water. It's from the big boys at Heileman. Are they Texans?

Colin: Its taste and style are sure to instantly remind you of Bud. That's not exactly a gripe, but it does have a rather trite flavor. Comes equipped with a fresh, very light golden color and somewhat weak head. Overall, a workmanlike job. 🍺🍺🍺

Randy: Almost colorless. You won't expect much after you pour, but there is flavor in there. Sour with a touch of bite. A few of these and I just might take up line dancing. 🍺🍺🍺

LONE STAR LIGHT

G. Heileman Brewing Co.
600 Lone Star Boulevard
San Antonio, Texas 78204
(210) 226-8301

Label Musings: Neat gold and white pinstripe with the "Lone" star right in the middle. The "National Beer of Texas." Did we miss something about a secession in the news recently?

Colin: If you want a distinctive or unique beer, this simply doesn't fit the bill. It describes itself as the "National Beer of Texas" and that seems to be the point. This was made to please the masses, the micro trappings notwithstanding.

Randy: At merely 110 calories, not a bad attempt. Still, though a consistent flavor for a light beer, it doesn't stand up to regulars. Perhaps we shouldn't compare apples to oranges. You make the choice.

LONE STAR NATURAL BOCK

G. Heileman Brewing Co.
600 Lone Star Boulevard
San Antonio, Texas 78204
(210) 226-8301

Label Musings: Of course, since it's a bock, there is a ram on the label. Wouldn't it be more appropriate for these Texans to add a little local flavor? Maybe a longhorn? Plus, this sheep looks like he's draggin' his keester.

Colin: It doesn't have the oomph usually found in a bock. Because I find lighter beers like lagers and pilsners more accessible anyhow, no demerits for that. But if you're looking for a great bock, look elsewhere.

Randy: Easy-going for a bock, with a mellow, smooth flavor, but a little sweeter than most. It's for the average beer drinker. When you're remembering the Alamo, remember to pick up a six-pack. Davy Crockett would be proud.

LORD CHESTERFIELD ALE

D.G. Yuengling & Son Inc.
P.O. Box 539
5th and Manhantongo Street
Pottsville, Pennsylvania 17901
(717) 622-4141

Label Musings: Long-necked green bottle with that chap Lord Chesterfield, one of the "famous" members of the British royal family (yeah, they know a lot about beer). Hey, this is America. No landed gentry here.

Colin: Its pale color masks a savory sweetness. The distinct taste clearly seems to be the result of a time-honored recipe. It's no accident. The beer comes from America's oldest brewers, as the label proudly proclaims. 🍺🍺🍺 ½

Randy: It's got "nose," which sometimes means the brew has a chemical taste. But I was pleasantly surprised. This is a light, smooth, drinkable brew. Make a scene by bringing a six-pack to the next royal function you attend. 🍺🍺🍺 ½

MANHATTAN GOLD LAGER

The Manhattan Brewing Co.
40-42 Thompson Street
New York, New York 10013
(212) 425-1515

Label Musings: The skyline of the Big Apple is prominent on a sapphire label. Has that big ad agency look to it. Probably one of them from right around the corner in trendy SoHo.

Colin: As Francis Albert belts it out better than anyone, if you can make it there, you'll make it anywhere. Manhattan Gold does just that. A robust flavor comes through, but it is controlled. Truly a "premium" bottle of beer. 🍺🍺🍺🍺

Randy: New Yorkers don't pull their punches and neither does this brew. But a brewery in Manhattan? I guess you can find anything in NYC. This lager has a full-bodied, dynamic flavor similar to an ale. 🍺🍺🍺 ½

MARKET STREET GOLDEN ALE

Bohannon Brewing Co.
134 Second Avenue North
Nashville, Tennessee 37201
(615) 242-8223

Label Musings: Turn-of-the-century sketch of what appears to be a cobblestoned Market Street. Reminds you of the opening to "Cheers."

Colin: Packs a much more potent taste than your run-of-the-mill golden ale. Not too overpowering to keep you from having more than one at a clip. Very satisfying and worthy of your patronage. 🍺🍺🍺

Randy: Here's something to imbibe on your way to the Grand Ol' Opry. Golden-colored and smooth but for me it's lacking in that crucial element: taste. There are lots better on the market. 🍺🍺

MARKET STREET PILSNER DRAFT

Bohannon Brewing Co.
134 Second Avenue North
Nashville, Tennessee 37201
(615) 242-8223

Label Musings: Same display as the Golden Ale, but it is golden and the Golden Ale is white. Go figure.

Colin: I detected an uncommon, nutty flavor. This is not likely to be your everyday beer. However, I highly recommend giving it a try as a nice change of pace or when you feel like treating yourself. 🍺🍺🍺🍺

Randy: The flavor that was missing from the Golden Ale seems to have turned up here. Lots of pop and hop. Take a leisurely stroll down Market Street. 🍺🍺🍺

MATT'S LIGHT PILSENER

F.X. Matt Brewing Co.
811 Edward Street
Utica, New York 13502
(315) 732-3181

Label Musings: The label is silver—increasingly the industry standard for packaging light beers. The label tells the story of the Matt family. Grandpa Matt used to brew for the famous Duke of Baden Brewery in the middle of the Black Forest. He settled in the Adirondacks and the family has kept the tradition going.

Colin: For a light beer, it is an impressive achievement. Of course, if it were judged as a regular strengthed beer, it would have its problems. On the light beer scale, it's OK with me.

Randy: The lowest calorie brew we have encountered to date at 87 calories. Unfortunately, it has that hops and water taste like so many others. I was rooting for this one because it was so low in calories. Maybe they should have left a few more of them in there. ¹/₂

McMAHON'S IRISH STYLE POTATO ALE

Minnesota Brewing Co.
882 West Seventh Street
St. Paul, Minnesota 55102
(612) 228-9173

Label Musings: Think St. Patty's Day and you won't miss this one on the shelf. You couldn't get more Irish if you were standing in the middle of Dublin reading James Joyce and listening to "Danny Boy" playing on the pipes.

Colin: Well, I didn't taste any potatoes in this brew and you'll get no complaints from me. I prefer my spuds baked with a little sour cream, not in my brewski. Whatever is in the recipe, the result is a mellow, unpretentious beer with a pleasing, consistent flavor. ¹/₂

Randy: Now here's a brand that should have a mascot named "Spuds." This odd potato brew is bitter, yet not harsh. If you're a meat and potatoes type, go for it.

McTARNAHAN'S ALE

Portland Brewing Company
2730 N.W. 31st Avenue
Portland, Oregon 97210
(503) 222-7150

Label Musings: They break out the tartan for this Scottish ale in green, blue and black. Sharp green and white bottlecap stamped "Mac's." It has earned a gold medal at the Great American Beer Festival for best American amber ale.

Colin: Creamy, sweet, but oh, so powerful, this Scottish ale is not easily forgotten. Serious beer drinkers will fully appreciate this masterpiece. Three cheers for this big Mac. 🍺🍺🍺🍺🍺

Randy: This stupendous, full-bodied beauty gives Grant's version of this variety a run for its money. Both are excellent, so take your pick. Get a six-pack and watch Brigadoon on the tube with a bonny lassie. 🍺🍺🍺🍺 ½

MICHAEL SHEA'S IRISH AMBER

Shea's Brewery
c/o The Genesee Brewing Co., Inc.
445 St. Paul Street
Rochester, New York 14605
(716) 546-1030

Label Musings: Look for the green and orange label with the Shea family crest. The saying "May the road rise to meet you, may the wind be always at your back" is a quaint touch. Gee, do you think Mr. Shea might be Irish?

Colin: The russet tones are bound to instantly remind you of an import, but it doesn't pack the same punch. With the packaging and a certain bitter taste, it is distinctive enough for me to give Mr. Shea polite applause, but no curtain call. 🍺🍺🍺

Randy: Amber-colored lager; no head and a little bitter for my tastes. I'm not impressed. But don't let Father Flannery hear me or I'll get booted from the Royal Order of the Hibernians. When is St. Patrick's Day? 🍺🍺

MR. MIKE'S LIGHT ALE

The New Haven Brewing Company
458 Grand Avenue
New Haven, Connecticut 06513
(203) 772-2739

Label Musings: Mr. Mike looks like a nut. What kind of bartender wears a candy-striped apron in this day and age? And why is he so happy? If you saw the movie Cocktail, you'll agree Mr. Mike is no Tom Cruise.

Colin: If you're gonna put your mug (both face and glass, that is) on the label, you should have something worth pushing. Although I understand that this is a light beer, it falls way short on taste. The label is certainly eye-catching, but the contents of the bottle will disappoint.

Randy: If this isn't fruit juice, I must have gone nutty like Mr. Mike. We all should watch our weight, but this light beer isn't worth it. Stick to lowfat milk and turkey kielbasa, but don't skimp on the brew unless you absolutely must.

NEUWEILER STOCK ALE

Neuweiler Brewing Co., Inc.
2310 S.W. 26th Street
Allentown, Pennsylvania 18103
(717) 767-3545 (The Lion Inc.)

Label Musings: What's with "Nix Besser" and a German eagle? The label looks like a Christmas greeting from the Reichstag. We welcome back this brewery, which returned to the market after more than a twenty-year absence. Their first run lasted from 1891 through 1968.

Colin: Dark, biting and overwhelmingly heavy, this is not for the faint of heart. I'm no wimp, but this overpowered me. I subtracted one "bottlecap" for the Euro-pandering label. ½

Randy: The label states that this concoction was brewed for their stockholders. I've never heard of the big beer companies paying dividends like this. It is bitter, but you can handle it. This powerful brew will stand up to any meal. However, it may lack mass appeal because of its potency. ½

NEW AMSTERDAM LIGHT AMBER BEER

The New Amsterdam Brewing Company
P.O. Box 1064
Old Chelsea Station
New York, New York 10113-0905
(315) 732-3181 (F.X. Matt Brewing Co.)

Label Musings: Painted bottle with clipper ship and large amber "LIGHT" under the brand name. If they can make a flavorful light beer, we'll buy it.

Colin: Kudos for the effort. It is essential that microbrewers put light versions on the scene if they're going to make a dramatic impact on the U.S. beer market. Unfortunately, this one won't blaze any trails. Recognizing that this is not an uncommon gripe against light beers, I still think the taste vanished with the calories.

Randy: It's 95 calories and made with Cascade and Hallertrauer hops. Unfortunately, it tastes like water and hops soup. It's a noble effort, but not for those of us who haven't been caught up in the aerobics fad. I say try, try again.

NEW AMSTERDAM NEW YORK ALE

The New Amsterdam Brewing Company
P.O. Box 1064
Old Chelsea Station
New York, New York 10113-0905
(315) 732-3181 (F.X. Matt Brewing Co.)

Label Musings: The clipper ship sails prominently on all of New Amsterdam's labels. This one is deep green. We're not sure why they christened this New Amsterdam New York Ale. History buffs know that they're two names for the same place.

Colin: It has a pleasant, but ordinary composition. With its strong aftertaste, this is a beer you'll most certainly remember. I propose that it may not be for the right reasons. 1/2

Randy: At first blush, this dry-hoppped, pale ale seems overwhelming. Frankly, my first reaction was, "Whoa, what the hell is this?" Then I got hit with the extremely bitter aftertaste. I can still taste it as I'm writing. 1/2

NEW AMSTERDAM NEW YORK AMBER

The New Amsterdam Brewing Company
P.O. Box 1064
Old Chelsea Station
New York, New York 10113-0905
(315) 732-3181 (F.X. Matt Brewing Co.)

Label Musings: The brewery sticks to its nautical theme in this gold and black combo. Classy, but totally uninspiring.

Colin: You'll find that nothing really stands out with this one. It lacks character, both in flavor and potency. Some beers seem to be stuck searching for a personality. This is one of them. 🍺 ½

Randy: This amber lager has a flowery twang. If you're partial to twang, it's for you. Although it's well-made, I wouldn't bring it to my friends at the bowling alley, if you know what I mean. 🍺🍺

NEW AMSTERDAM WINTER ANNIVERSARY

The New Amsterdam Brewing Company
P.O. Box 1064
Old Chelsea Station
New York, New York 10113-0905
(315) 732-3181 (F.X. Matt Brewing Co.)

Label Musings: High art formally enters the beer world with this abstract label painting entitled "Orrah" by Tobi Kahn. There is a quote by the artist that may make less sense to you than some beer reviewers.

Colin: Deep hue, but not much taste. While undeniably smooth, if you seek a robust, hearty beer, you can do better. Brewed to mark the anniversary of the founding of the city of New Amsterdam in 1624. Some occasions may best be forgotten. 🍺🍺

Randy: I think these brewers have lost track of the beer in their pursuit of artistic endeavors. Where's the taste in this winter ale? I didn't even appreciate the artwork on the label. This one's not worth bidding on. 🍺

NEW ENGLAND ATLANTIC AMBER

New England Brewing Company, Inc.
25 Commerce Street
Norwalk, Connecticut 06852
(203) 866-1339

Label Musings: Yet another beer label depicting a clipper ship? Give us a locomotive, a spaceship, even a bus. But please, we beg all brewers, no more clipper ships battling the mighty Atlantic!

Colin: Malt, malt, malt. I'm not talking about those delicious chocolate malts you might have in a '50's-style diner with your sweetheart. I'm talking about beer. It overwhelms this otherwise pleasant brewski. 🍺🍺

Randy: Extremely fruity, and, yes, malty. But not terribly malty. Remember that beer tasting is highly subjective, so if you're fanatical about hearty, malty brews, go for it. 🍺🍺

NEW ENGLAND GOLD STOCK ALE

New England Brewing Company, Inc.
25 Commerce Street
Norwalk, Connecticut 06852
(203) 866-1339

Label Musings: A gold label and guess what's on it? A clipper ship, you say? You're a genius.

Colin: This ale comes with an aftertaste that hits you before you even swallow. That's a bit too much for me. Bitter and downright difficult to drink, I don't recommend you spend your hard-earned dough on this forgettable brew. 🍺

Randy: I can't imagine it finding an audience because it is so bitter and sour. The Charles Barkley of beers: it dares you to like it and it's no role model. 🍺

NEW ENGLAND HOLIDAY ALE

New England Brewing Company, Inc.
25 Commerce Street
Norwalk, Connecticut 06852
(203) 866-1339

Label Musings: Cranberry background with gold clipper ship. Very original, don't you think?

Colin: This holiday specialty beer seems to have been brewed with Ebeneezer Scrooge in mind. Bitter and exceedingly sour, it's not likely to put you in a festive mood. 🍺 ½

Randy: This sour concoction almost ruined my holidays. It's got a mouthwash quality that's sure to give you the blues. Who needs that? 🍺

NEW ENGLAND OATMEAL STOUT

New England Brewing Company, Inc.
25 Commerce Street
Norwalk, Connecticut 06852
(203) 866-1339

Label Musings: Standard New England Brewing Company label (by that we mean a clipper ship!), this time in metallic green. Is drinking this beer the "right thing to do"? Read on.

Colin: Wilford Brimley would be in heaven. Basically a stout, with a tinge of oatmeal. Even with the use of oatmeal, you'll find little unique about this brew. Maybe you can have a couple for a liquid breakfast come next St. Patty's Day. 🍺🍺

Randy: Opaque and bitter with a silky consistency. Full of hearty, robust flavor. A stout lover's stout. You can hardly taste any oatmeal, so if you're looking for a healthy way to start your day, stick with cornflakes. 🍺🍺🍺

NEW YORK HARBOR DARK ALE

Old World Brewing Company, Inc.
2070 Victory Boulevard
Staten Island, New York 10314
(718) 370-0551

Label Musings: The beloved Brooklyn Bridge as seen from the South Street Seaport of Manhattan. Patriotic slogan "Brewed with pride in the USA."

Colin: Piquant and sturdy. If you like your java black, you may latch on to this one. With its ominous look, you'd expect it to have more flavor. For those of you accustomed to bland pilsners but game for something a bit more exotic, this may be a solid choice. 🍺🍺🍺 ¹/₂

Randy: Another glass stainer! It has a burnt, yet sweet flavor. This ale's color is deep and extremely dark, which may remind you of porters. It may only be for the heartiest drinkers among us. Master brewer Sal Pennacchio is a soul mate. 🍺🍺🍺 ¹/₂

NEWMAN'S ALBANY AMBER

The Newman Brewing Co.
84 Chestnut Street
Albany, New York 12210
(518) 465-8501

Label Musings: Moustached rower from the turn of the century is depicted in full stroke. He's probably heading to a riverside saloon for a refreshment.

Colin: A hearty amber beer. Nothing fancy, just a full, zesty taste without bitterness and sans any disagreeable aftertaste. No small achievement. Be forewarned, it possesses an ale's potency, but it's worth it. 🍺🍺🍺 ¹/₂

Randy: This Albany amber is in the Viennese style. Hoppy enough for a jack rabbit. It has a middling, malty, sweet taste that certain aficionados might appreciate, but it's not for everyone. 🍺🍺 ¹/₂

NEWMAN'S SARATOGA LAGER

The Newman Brewing Co.
84 Chestnut Street
Albany, New York 12210
(518) 465-8501

Label Musings: The depicted thoroughbred is off to the races in full gallop. A fitting label for a beer named Saratoga, home of one of the nation's oldest and perhaps most beautiful racetracks. See you at the two dollar window.

Colin: This lager has a pale, dry taste with a hint of tang. A sweet taste makes it more than a mediocre beer. I'm taking a cooler to a day at the races. Even if I lose my shirt, I'll be happy. 🍺🍺🍺

Randy: Potent for a lager, with a sweet, sharp, full flavor. I had high expectations after taking in the handsome label, but I think this brew came up lame. No Triple Crown winner here. 🍺🍺

NIGHTWATCH DARK ALE

Maritime Pacific Brewing Co.
1514 Northwest Leary Way
Seattle, Washington 98107
(206) 782-6181

Label Musings: Clipper ship motif on a label that proclaims "Brewed in the Northwest with Imagination." Perhaps the imagination was exhausted in brewing the beer. Certainly none was used designing this label.

Colin: I think they brewed this one in the dark. Or maybe some part-time nightwatchman doubles as the brewmaster. Whatever the reason, this one doesn't do it for me. I don't recommend it for your beer drinking pleasure, during the day, at night or at any time in between. 🍺

Randy: Brother, the label was right. The brewers who put this together perhaps have an overactive imagination. Overwhelmingly bitter and sour. Turn out the lights, the party's over. 🍺

OKTOBERFEST ALE

North Coast Brewing Co.
444 North Main Street
Fort Bragg, California 95437
(707) 964-BREW

Label Musings: Autumn leaf on an ecru background with German-styled "Oktoberfest" in maroon. Makes you feel like breaking out your favorite sweater.

Colin: An ale that lives up to its billing. To its credit, it doesn't try to split the difference in order to appeal to a larger audience. Plenty of flavor and plenty of bite. If you stock up on this stuff, autumn will quickly become your favorite season. 🍺🍺🍺

Randy: This hearty, spicy ale should make the Germans green with envy. If you are so inclined, put on some lederhosen, wind the cuckoo clock and invite over an oom-pah band to play a few ditties. Then break out this brew. The party's bound to last for days. 🍺🍺🍺🍺

OLD DETROIT AMBER ALE

The Old Detroit Brewing Co.
Frankenmuth Brewery
425 South Main Street
Frankenmuth, Michigan 48734
(517) 652-6183

Label Musings: If you call yourself "Old Detroit," you've got to put a classic automobile on the label. And that's just what they did. A sharp Model T in eye-catching red, white and blue.

Colin: Detroit is a tough town, filled with sharp-elbowed folks and epitomized by former Piston Bill Laimbeer. Well, this lame beer doesn't quite capture that same spirit. It's syrupy sweet and lacks that hint of harshness that you've come to expect and enjoy from traditional ales. 🍺🍺

Randy: The sweetness of this ale will start your engine. There's a tremendous hop potency that I believe most are likely to find unpleasant. Has Motown lost its edge? Even if you pass on this one, remember, buy American! 🍺🍺

OLD NO. 38 STOUT

North Coast Brewing Co.
444 North Main Street
Fort Bragg, California 95437
(707) 964-2739

Label Musings: Old No. 38 is seen chuggin' along and you too can chug out of the 22-ounce bottle (if you can handle it). If you look closely, you'll spy a whale tail.

Colin: On first impression, you may think this stuff is used to power Old No. 38. This stout is thick and black. Like a heavy locomotive, it takes a while to get going. When it does, you'll agree that there's something about a train that's, well, magic. 🍺🍺🍺 ½

Randy: As I drank this heavy brew I kept saying, "I think I can, I think I can, I know I can." Brawny stout has all the flavor and creaminess you can imagine. Old No. 38 keeps rolling along, since 1987. Pitch some more coal and pop open another bottle. 🍺🍺🍺🍺

OLD PECONIC HAMPTON ALE

The Old Peconic Brewing Company, Ltd.
21A Congdon Road
P.O. Box 758
Shelter Island, New York 11964
(516) 749-8823

Label Musings: Blue, yellow and white background with a sketch of a lighthouse. The label declares that the brewers are dedicated to preserving Long Island, New York's natural resources. Hey, we all need a hobby.

Colin: A strong, biting flavor marks this otherwise pleasant ale. It has a fresh, clean taste that makes you appreciate the brewer's efforts. When the clubs in Southhampton stock this stuff, the folks out there will really start living the good life. 🍺🍺🍺 ½

Randy: It is supposed to taste like the brew prepared by English settlers living on Long Island three hundred years ago. I always thought life was hard back then. With this robust, elegant and evenly-brewed ale, it just couldn't have been that rough. 🍺🍺🍺🍺

OLDE HEURICH MAERZEN BEER

The Olde Heurich Brewing Co.
1111 34th Street, N.W.
Washington, D.C. 20007
(202) 333-2313

Label Musings: The goateed Christian Heurich's contented smirk says almost as much as the upper label's tombstone-like description of the brew's history. A lot of pride went into this one.

Colin: D.C. fancies itself a "capital" city and it has a beer to match its self-importance. This beer delivers on its boasts. A vivid amber hue and a satisfying European-style taste combine to provide a memorable drinking experience. With this beer available locally, it's no wonder nothing ever gets done in that town. 🍺🍺🍺🍺 ½

Randy: Hearty, potent ale but easy enough on the palate. It's not hard to figure out why this beer has been a favorite since 1873. Just consider how many presidents, ambassadors and visiting royalty may have sampled this brew. And how many of them that probably got bombed. 🍺🍺🍺🍺

OLDENBERG BLONDE LIGHT

Oldenberg Brewing Company
I-75 at 400 Buttermilk Pike
Fort Mitchell, Kentucky 41017
(606) 341-2800

Label Musings: Royal blue and gold. No blonde. No brunette. This is the first brew we've seen that has touted a silver medal at the Great American Beer Festival. What's next, honorable mention?

Colin: One of the few light beers with more taste than air and a surprisingly potent flavor. If you've got to go light, go with a blonde. It's more fun. 🍺🍺🍺🍺

Randy: I'm not sure how many calories it has, but I am sure that there is a whole lot of flavor for a light beer. Despite being a light, this beer stands on its own. Remember, gentlemen prefer blondes. 🍺🍺🍺 ½

OLDENBERG OPV

Oldenberg Brewing Company
I-75 at 400 Buttermilk Pike
Fort Mitchell, Kentucky 41017
(606) 341-2800

Label Musings: The splendid green and gold label has a red sash proclaiming "OPV" at the bottom. You down with OPV? Yeah, you know me.

Colin: The German tradition comes through loud and clear. Oldenberg easily matches or surpasses the best imports from Deutschland. If you're still patronizing the foreign brands, this one should compel you to reclaim your heritage. Hooray for the red, white and blue! 🍺🍺🍺🍺

Randy: I consider myself as patriotic as they come, but among great American beers, it doesn't make the honor roll. Unfortunately, it seems a little light on its feet. This pale ale possesses a fruity flavor that doesn't hit a home run. 🍺🍺 ½

OLDENBERG WEISS WHEAT BEER

Oldenberg Brewing Company
I-75 at 400 Buttermilk Pike
Fort Mitchell, Kentucky 41017
(606) 341-2800

Label Musings: Stocky bottle with a colorful label emblazoned with "WEISS." Amazingly, you can hardly see the name Oldenberg in white on the silver background. C'mon guys. With so many brands now on the shelf, this one could get lost in the shuffle.

Colin: While an admirable effort, it likely won't set the American wheat beer standard. Passable, but the wheat flavor doesn't leap out at you. If you're cruising down I-75, stop off and pick up a sample. 🍺🍺

Randy: Sweeter than most wheat beers, it has a frisky, flowery aftertaste. Wheat beer has the potential to become incredibly popular among American drinkers; however, this attempt will not likely inspire the masses. 🍺🍺

OLDENBERG WINTER ALE

Oldenberg Brewing Company
I-75 at 400 Buttermilk Pike
Fort Mitchell, Kentucky 41017
(606) 341-2800

Label Musings: Gorgeous, fairy tale inspired illustration of a star-filled winter sky with Old Man Winter blowing up an icy wind. If ever there were a beer worth buying simply to admire its label, this could well be it.

Colin: This beer is chock full of flavor, but the effect isn't terribly pleasing. It has an overpowering tanginess that didn't agree with me. Break it out only for the most severe cold snaps. 🍺🍺

Randy: Self-proclaimed brewmaster Ken Schienberg pledges that "you will find this hearty Ale to be a masterpiece of the brewer's art." It's not quite as smashing as touted, but it is spicy and tart. There is a bitter aftertaste. 🍺🍺🍺

PEARL LAGER BEER

Pearl Brewing Co.
312 Pearl Parkway
P.O. Box 1661
San Antonio, Texas 78296
(210) 226-0231

Label Musings: The vintage label reminds us of the beers our fathers drank. No Rembrandt here. Definitely one to peel, if you catch our drift. Try to decode the message hidden under the bottlecap.

Colin: A light, smooth brew from down Texas way. It has a fine, mellow style, so you can really knock them back. String a few of these together and you'll have your own private hoedown. I once courted a filly named Pearl, but that's another story. 🍺🍺🍺 ½

Randy: My initial thought was "I can drink this, and a lot of it." Get yourself a cold mug on a hot day after a solid day's work and kick back. It's from San Antonio, but it could be from a brew capital like Milwaukee or St. Louis. Nothing's lost in the translation. 🍺🍺🍺 ½

PENN PILSNER

Pennsylvania Brewing Company
800 Vinial Street
Pittsburgh, Pennsylvania 15212
(412) 237-9400

Label Musings: Sketch of the old Allegheny Brewery, complete with smokestacks that harken back to the industrial revolution and Pennsylvanians like Andrew Carnegie. Don't they know we're in the environmentally-conscious '90s?

Colin: The Keystone State has many things to be proud of, but I venture that this forgettable offering is not among them. If a pilsner is what you crave, the roster is brimming with more worthwhile brews. 🪙 $1/2$

Randy: "Gebraut aus Hopfen und Malz, Hefe und Wasser, Reinheit mit Garantie." What the hell is that? Our translator tells us it guarantees the beer's purity. Well, at least the label indicates in English that there are no fillers such as corn or rice used. Smooth, sour and not particularly interesting. 🪙 $1/2$

PERRY'S MAJESTIC

The Riverosa Brewing Company Inc.
101 West 75th Street
New York, New York
(212) 721-4566

Label Musings: Drab, red "P" over a black background. Did Perry earn his varsity letter in brewing studies? The label crows the beer is made from organically grown barley and hops. Oh, isn't that just so precious?

Colin: Not even a hint of bitterness in this lager, but I don't find it "majestic." I recommend it only for those few beer drinkers out there who are afraid of pesticides. 🪙🪙

Randy: The organic concept conjures up thoughts of half-naked hippies wallowing in the mud, stoned on God-knows-what and listening to some other naked, stoned maniacs banging away on their bongos in a field in upstate New York. But I digress. This is pretty tasty stuff. Too bad it's organic. 🪙🪙🪙

PETE'S GOLD COAST LAGER

Pete's Brewing Co.
514 High Street
Palo Alto, California 94301
(800) 877-PETE

Label Musings: View of longshoremen unloading brew at a 19th-century port. The faded colors make it hard to discern. Pete's sneering puss is there, too.

Colin: A lager that really comes across as a potent ale. This ripe brew is distinctive and packed with flavor. Because Pete's brands are becoming more readily available, you'll probably wind up trying it soon if you haven't already. You won't be disappointed. 🍺🍺🍺 ¹/₂

Randy: It's a smooth and even lager. There's a load of sweet, even taste. Beware, easy drinkability is bound to lead to heavy intake. Probably similar to the stuff the fellas on Cannery Row used to throw back. 🍺🍺🍺 ¹/₂

PETE'S WICKED ALE

Pete's Brewing Co.
514 High Street
Palo Alto, California 94301
(800) 877-PETE

Label Musings: Nautical accents, including the boast, "America's premier microbrewery." They talk the talk, but can they walk the walk?

Colin: A potent brew, but you can handle it. I don't want to sound like a cliche or a beer commercial (too often the same thing), but the quality really does come through. Try it, for Pete's sake. You'll be glad you did. 🍺🍺🍺🍺

Randy: This "chocolate malt" of ales has an extremely dark color and roasted, caramel qualities. It has a smooth, easy-going gusto, yet is even keeled. Buy some for a friend who's not yet weaned off the bigger brands. Guaranteed, it'll open their eyes. 🍺🍺🍺🍺 ¹/₂

PETE'S WICKED LAGER

Pete's Brewing Co.
514 High Street
Palo Alto, California 94301
(800) 877-PETE

Label Musings: Similar to the Wicked Ale. A large "Wicked" and Pete's sneer. What do they mean by "wicked"? Is that wicked in a good sense? A huge advertising and distribution push has put this brew on everyone's lips.

Colin: Pete, you ain't so bad. From such an intimidating moniker, I expected to be bowled over. Although this beer is mild, it more than holds its own. It doesn't take home a gold medal, but it should be taken seriously. 🍺🍺🍺 ½

Randy: Thick head and complex flavor. This microbrew could eventually be mass marketed—but then will it still be a microbrew? Sample a fresh bottle of this stuff and then drink an import and tell me which is better. Believe me, it's no contest. 🍺🍺🍺🍺

PIG'S EYE PILSNER

Minnesota Brewing Co.
882 West Seventh Street
St. Paul, Minnesota 55102
(612) 228-9173

Label Musings: One-eyed, ornery old salt scowling at you like you've just been condemned to walk the plank. By the way, Pig's Eye is the nickname for St. Paul, Minnesota.

Colin: Not laden with taste; actually it's on the tepid side. Very drinkable, but you could tire of it easily if you're hankering for a brew with heft. 🍺🍺

Randy: Pilsner that doesn't deliver the goods. What flavor there is tends to be bitter and sour. Not very appealing. Don't be plundered by this pirate and lose your hard-earned booty. 🍺

PIKE PLACE PALE ALE

Pike Place Brewery
1432 Western Avenue
Seattle, Washington 98101
(206) 622-3373

Label Musings: This distinctive, painted long-neck bottle exhibits a big white diamond with red and transparent lettering. The six-pack case solemnly reminds us that "Micro-brew is a philosophy, a respect for the tradition and culture of brewing one of the world's oldest food products." It's O.K., you can cry, you're among friends.

Colin: Its potent flavor and bold aftertaste may not make it your beer of choice. Personally, I'm having three with dinner tonight. I picked up some Dungeness crabs at the fantastic Pike Place Market in Seattle. Now that's good eatin'. 🍺🍺🍺

Randy: With hints of barley, you'll find it's capably done, but not quite as good as other available Seattle ales. You should give it a try during a ferry ride across Puget Sound. 🍺🍺 ½

PORTLAND TRADITIONAL LAGER

Coastal Brewing
200 High Street
Boston, Massachusetts 02220
(617) 439-7727

Label Musings: Simple lighthouse and sailboat. Makes you want to head out to the shore.

Colin: This brew has character and personality (like most beer drinkers). Comes equipped with a subtle flavor and ruddy color. It really has it all, and no gimmicks. 🍺🍺🍺 ½

Randy: Although it's from Boston, it is named "Portland." Is that Maine or Oregon? The lighthouse must have been out. There is no body to be found in this watery grave. At least they have a stamp of approval from the Lighthouse Preservation Society. 🍺🍺

PUMPKIN ALE

Buffalo Bill's Brewery
1082 B Street
Hayward, California 94541
(510) 886-9823

Label Musings: Giant pumpkin doubling as a vat with Bill stirring up his special potion. Bright orange and green colors. Is it the "Great Pumpkin"?

Colin: If you like pumpkin pie (or even if you don't), give this very original, interesting beer a try. You'll agree that beer lovers will make it a fall tradition. Destined to become as eagerly anticipated as the stuffed bird on Turkey Day. It'll bring a smile to your face and put color in your cheeks. 🍺🍺🍺🍺

Randy: It's fermented with pumpkin! Quite a novelty, but not just for Halloween. It has a spicy bite and a sweet aftertaste. Hooray for American brewing innovations. What's next? Broccoli beer? That's where I draw the line. 🍺🍺🍺🍺

PYRAMID AMBER WHEATEN

Hart Brewing, Inc.
P.O. Box 1179
Kalama, Washington 98625
(206) 673-2962

Label Musings: Pyramids in the woods of the Pacific Northwest. You gotta love the incongruity of the scene. The label boasts "quaffability" and claims it is a "fine complement to shellfish, salads and other summer fare." Fare? What's wrong with just saying grub? We are talking about beer here.

Colin: A zesty, tangy wheat beer with a hint of clove in the aftertaste. Wheat beer fans will quickly notice that this isn't a lemonade-style wheat beer. For non-wheat drinkers, it's well worth your while as an introductory primer. 🍺🍺🍺 ½

Randy: This Dunkelweizen-style, dark wheat beer has considerable potency and, dare I say, quaffability. Not one of the best Pyramids, but I'd give it a shot as a curiosity. 🍺🍺 ½

PYRAMID BEST BROWN ALE

Hart Brewing, Inc.
P.O. Box 1179
Kalama, Washington 98625
(206) 673-2962

Label Musings: This brew has won a gold medal at the Great American Beer Festival as best brown ale, so have a little respect. Green and yellow rays emanate from the centrally located Great Pyramid. Maybe it's the tomb of a revered beer baron from another epoch.

Colin: More amber than brown, so don't be scared off. Done with great flair. I highly recommend this very appealing beer which is brimming with flavor. You don't have to be an archaeologist to dig this one.
◖◗◖◗

Randy: This isn't a pyramid as much as it is a diamond, and not one in the rough either. A marvelous, stylish brown ale with a full body and malt flavor. I've unearthed a treasure. *◖◗◖◗* ¹/₂

PYRAMID HEFEWEIZEN ALE

Hart Brewing, Inc.
P.O. Box 1179
Kalama, Washington 98625
(206) 673-2962

Label Musings: Darker brown label than Pyramid Wheaten Ale denotes the use of yeast in the recipe. Hefeweizen means a style of wheat beer brewed with yeast. A German toast is offered: "Prosit!"

Colin: Quite a novel brew. Its flaxen, yellow head will remind you of lemon meringue pie. It tastes almost as tart. A nice change of pace. *◖◗◖◗*

Randy: Label directs you to "carefully pour all but two fingers of Hefeweizen into your glass. Vigorously swirl remainder while chanting 'Pyramid Hefeweizen' three times. Pour to the last drop." The day there's only a drop of this stuff left will be a sad day indeed. Simply world class. *◖◗◖◗◖*

PYRAMID PALE ALE

Hart Brewing, Inc.
P.O. Box 1179
Kalama, Washington 98625
(206) 673-2962

Label Musings: The label states that the "first bottled versions of English bitters were paler than the porter style draft beers of the day, hence the name 'Pale Ale.'" It is recommended to be enjoyed with veal, game birds and Cajun and Mexican cuisine. Here we go again with the beer as a complement to dinner stuff. No need for the high hat. A burger and a good brew is about as gourmet as it gets.

Colin: Not very pale for a pale ale. It has a real edge to it and no shortage of flavor. A sure bet for ale addicts. In deference to the label suggestion, I'm going out to buy some game birds to complement this beer. 🍺🍺🍺 ¹/₂

Randy: Bitter yet smooth. A miraculous achievement from the folks at Hart Brewing. I'm a believer in Pyramid Power. Remember, an ale on the bitter side may not be for everyone, but all can appreciate this special beverage. 🍺🍺🍺🍺

PYRAMID SPHINX STOUT

Hart Brewing, Inc.
P.O. Box 1179
Kalama, Washington 98625
(206) 673-2962

Label Musings: No pyramid in this forest, but, low and behold, there's a sphinx instead. If the ancient Egyptians had brew the caliber of the Pyramid brands, the pharaohs might still be in charge over there.

Colin: Disappointing, dark, sweet stout. Not quite one of the Seven Wonders. Very predictable, with nothing to particularly set it apart from the rest. 🍺🍺

Randy: Black as night, or maybe blacker. This stout is a conversation starter at the very least. I doubt you can finish more than one at a time, but you'll have a memorable time trying. Replete with flavor. 🍺🍺🍺 ¹/₂

PYRAMID WHEATEN ALE

Hart Brewing, Inc.
P.O. Box 1179
Kalama, Washington 98625
(206) 673-2962

Label Musings: Bright yellow which, like the whole Pyramid line, certainly stands out. Red and green lettering and border distinguish this one from the crowded field.

Colin: Crisp, light and very refreshing, but don't worry, there's plenty of taste in the bottle as well. Ask yourself whether Cleopatra would have reached for that asp if she could have reached for a Pyramid instead. 🍺🍺🍺 ½

Randy: The Pyramid line features numerous beer styles with wheat added. In most cases, this imaginative approach works. However, this one misses the mark. The wheat further confuses an already complicated flavor. 🍺🍺 ½

PYRAMID WHEATEN BOCK

Hart Brewing, Inc.
P.O. Box 1179
Kalama, Washington 98625
(206) 673-2962

Label Musings: Sage green background and bottlecap. As with so many other bocks, there is a ram on the label. It's precariously perched on the familiar pyramid. Hope he doesn't fall. For you trivia buffs, the label informs us that the bock style of beer originated in the Bavarian city of Einbeck.

Colin: Despite the added element of wheat, it tastes like other bocks, but it's a dandy. Bock beer is traditionally served on the first day of spring. At the first sign of those swallows returning to Capistrano, I'm tapping the keg. 🍺🍺🍺🍺

Randy: This is an easy-to-drink, mild bock. The wheat takes some of the sting out of it. Dense and dulcet. Forget about goats, this brew is a hero in my book. 🍺🍺🍺 ½

RATTLESNAKE BEER

**Kershenstine's Diamond Beer Co.
3792 Veterans Memorial Boulevard
New Orleans, Louisiana 70119
(504) 888-7000**

Label Musings: Clear bottle with a gargantuan rattlesnake. Also, a picture of Pappy Kershenstine. He looks as if he was quite a character in his day.

Colin: Don't be fooled by the clever name. This beer doesn't bite and it sure isn't lethal. Tastes like a light beer. Maybe it's brewed with a desert climate in mind, where the rattlesnake roams. Maybe it's just using a catchy name to sell a tepid brew. My intuition points to the latter. 🍺 ½

Randy: The label urges "Get Bit!" This rattlesnake reminds me more of an inchworm. Believe me, there isn't much bite in the bottle. Even snake-fearing Indiana Jones wouldn't be intimidated by this tame stuff. Watery and uneven. Perhaps you can make a good gumbo with this Louisiana concoction. 🍺 ½

RED DAWG ALE

**Onalaska Brewing Co.
248 Burchett Road
Onalaska, Washington 98570
(206) 978-4253**

Label Musings: Affectionate and apparently toothless husky dog is the highlight of this amusing label. Sharp red, gold and black color scheme stands out.

Colin: A delightful, delicate flavor for an ale. Its rich taste and smooth body come together in this most satisfying brew. This dog is too friendly to bite you. Maybe just a nibble. 🍺🍺🍺🍺

Randy: There is an abundance of flavor in this hearty red ale. Why put a gummy husky on the label when you're pushing a beer with real teeth in it? Beats me. 🍺🍺🍺 ½

RED FEATHER PALE ALE

Arrowhead Brewing Co.
1667 Orchard Drive
Chambersburg, Pennsylvania 17201
(717) 264-0101

Label Musings: The label has a big, red feather.
How original.

Colin: Call off the cavalry. This mild ale is a pussycat.
To hell with the peace pipe, this tepid concoction is
sure to mellow any crowd. 🍺 ¹/₂

Randy: Reddish color and light as a feather. At least
the label is accurate. I prefer my beer to hit me like a
ton of bricks. Further, its odor, dare I say, is a bit
unpleasant. 🍺 ¹/₂

RED MOUNTAIN GOLDEN ALE

Birmingham Brewing Company
3118 3rd Avenue South
Birmingham, Alabama 35233
(205) 326-6677

Label Musings: An outdoorsman atop Red Mountain
hoists a spear skyward. This brewery has revived the
Alabama brewing tradition of its predecessor name-
sake, which closed in 1908 after the enactment of
statewide prohibition.

Colin: If you are looking for a refreshing taste in a
premium beer, but don't want to sacrifice drinkability,
your search is over. The folks at Red Mountain have
come up with a winner. 🍺🍺🍺🍺

Randy: The label says it is steam brewed in the
English tradition. That may be a lot of hot air. For a
beer that supposedly has Southern charm, I found it
particularly bitter and uninviting. 🍺🍺

RED MOUNTAIN RED ALE

Birmingham Brewing Company
3118 3rd Avenue South
Birmingham, Alabama 35233
(205) 326-6677

Label Musings: Same set-up as the Golden Ale, but
the background is red rather than blue. Don't get them
confused because they're quite different. The label
explains, "Be satisfied knowing that you're drinking
the finest beer available in Birmingham." Wow!

Colin: Certainly ranks near the top of the red ales on
the market. Boasts a reddish tint and a crisp, polished
taste. Another champ from the Birmingham bunch.
🍺🍺🍺🍺 ½

Randy: These guys have been brewing since 1992, so
they have "tons" of experience. This red ale is virtually
transparent. You can see the bottom of your glass.
Despite that, it is brimming with potent, sharp flavor. It is
somewhat bitter and has a lingering aftertaste. 🍺🍺 ½

RED NECTAR ALE

Humboldt Brewing Company
856 Tenth Street
Arcata, California 95521
(707) 826-2739

Label Musings: Nifty artwork featuring a humming-
bird collecting nectar from mountain flora. You won't
want to miss it. Former Oakland Raiders player Mario
Celotto owns the joint. NFL veteran and now
microbrewer. Is this a great country or what?

Colin: Don't let the charming picture on the label fool
you. This is an ale through and through, which I am
sure many folks won't mind a bit. It is robust, yet
consistent with an intriguing, red color and just a
touch of bitterness. 🍺🍺🍺 ½

Randy: At first glance, the appearance of a rusty,
murky broth turned me off. How appearances can be
deceiving! This foamy-headed, ambrosial nectar is OK
by me. It's a real humm-dinger. 🍺🍺🍺🍺

RED TAIL ALE

Mendocino Brewing Co.
P.O. Box 400
Hopland, California 95449
(707) 744-1015

Label Musings: Spectacular hawk carrying barley and hops. I guess that's the tastiest prey available in Hopland.

Colin: No surprises here. Satisfying, but totally conventional red ale. The striking label may drive you to succumb. A solid, worthy effort that doesn't quite soar. 🍺🍺 ¹/₂

Randy: I want to catch the next train to Hopland. This crisp, brazen ale is nevertheless approachable for beer lovers of all persuasions. I'm with that hawk. Who needs field mice anyway? 🍺🍺🍺🍺

REDHOOK ESB ALE

The Redhook Ale Brewery
3400 Phinney Avenue North
Seattle, Washington 98103
(206) 548-8000

Label Musings: The funky print on the label looks almost oriental; like signs at shops in Chinatown. Those trolley guys on the incongruous upper label look glum. Somebody get them some cold ones, quick!

Colin: ESB stands for extra special bitter, so I knew what I was in for. Left me completely embittered. Skip it unless you are into such flavors. It's just not for me. 🍺 ¹/₂

Randy: It's bitter all right. You've got to be in the right mood to go for this one. Just lose your job? Girlfriend split? Your favorite team lose the World Series? Your dog die? If not, you may not want to sour your mood. 🍺 ¹/₂

RHINO CHASERS AMERICAN ALE

William & Scott Co.
8460 Higuera Street
Culver City, California 90232
(800) 788-HORN

Label Musings: Red, white and blue rhinoceros head superimposed on the Liberty Bell. Is nothing sacred? The label announces that it is the only American ale as "elegant as a lager with the richness of an ale." We'll see about that.

Colin: Hits the palate a little too hard. Clean and crisp, but this ale is supposed to be brewed for humans, not for beasts roaming the plains of Africa. It's likely to make it to the endangered species list.

Randy: Smooth, light-tasting ale. Doesn't exactly charge at you like a rhino, but that's not a letdown. I am confounded by the name of the beer, which claims to support the African Wildlife Foundation. Why isn't it named "Rhino Lovers"?

RHINO CHASERS LAGER BEER

William & Scott Co.
8460 Higuera Street
Culver City, California 90232
(800) 788-HORN

Label Musings: Orange background this time for our familiar, friendly Rhino. As the label points out, a majority of the profits goes to the African Wildlife Foundation. Buy a case and you might just be saving the life of one of those magnificent beasts. Just something to think about next time you consider picking up a case of a big, corporate brand. All that will do is make the fat cats a little fatter.

Colin: Delivers a clean, mellow taste. It could very well become a popular everyday brew for many. Ride herd over to the supermarket, chase down a six-pack and see if you agree. 1/2

Randy: Sour and not particularly engaging. This rhino has seen better days. Perhaps you should donate directly to the AWF and take a charitable contribution deduction on your tax form. 1/2

ROCK & ROLL BEER

Rock & Roll Beer Co.
6504 Delmar
St. Louis, Missouri 63130
(314) 727-0110

Label Musings: The '50's era jukebox is playing, the beer is flowing. . . what could be better? As the label shouts, "Party"!

Colin: Why bother? Don't fall prey to the fancy label and the allure of rock & roll. You're smarter than that, aren't you? Elvis may forever be the king of rock & roll, but this ain't the king of beers. 🍺 1/2

Randy: A very drinkable brew. Bland for a brew named after rock & roll. Have you noticed there are no beers named after classical music, rap or country? So far, just jazz and rock. 🍺🍺 1/2

ROGUE ALE

Oregon Brewing Co.
2320 OSU Drive
Newport, Oregon 97365
(503) 867-3660

Label Musings: This rogue guy means business. No words grace the label except "Rogue Ale" and a miserable ruffian. The brew is "dedicated to the Rogue in all of us." The 12-ounce bottles are key when you're not up to a 22-ounce dose.

Colin: Its sharply potent flavor will be a bit too overwhelming to most. However, this ale does possess a certain self-assuredness. Ale addicts should be sure to try it. 🍺🍺 1/2

Randy: In my opinion, it tastes like bitter, vegetable broth. If this Rogue challenged me to a shoot-out, I'd meet that sucker any time, any place. 🍺

ROGUE GOLDEN ALE

Oregon Brewing Co.
2320 OSU Drive
Newport, Oregon 97365
(503) 867-3660

Label Musings: Snazzy, yellow swashbuckler painted on a 22-ounce brown bottle. The description of the brew on the back indicates that it's brewed in the pre-Prohibition tradition with at least 60 pounds of malt per barrel. Malty.

Colin: Obliging, affable flavor and very drinkable. You'll get a kick out of the herbs detectable in the aftertaste. Not your typical golden ale by any means.
🍺🍺🍺🍺

Randy: Fresh-tasting, with a discernable, full, hoppy flavor, and a tart aftertaste. Pull a cold one out of the fridge and chill out with this refreshing Rogue.
🍺🍺🍺🍺

ROGUE MEXICALI ALE

Oregon Brewing Co.
2320 OSU Drive
Newport, Oregon 97365
(503) 867-3660

Label Musings: Painted bottle with friendly guy from south of the border in front of a green cactus. Gotta love those painted bottles. Well worth saving in the attic. When are you gonna start a collection?

Colin: The aftertaste hits you like a spicy salsa. Very drinkable and original. Whip up a platter of nachos, add a couple of these 22-ounce bottles and you've got yourself an instant fiesta. 🍺🍺🍺🍺

Randy: Unlike Ed's Cave Creek, this brew has no floating chili pepper. However, the use of Chipatle chilis spices up the mixture. It has a sweet start and a peppery finish. Less insane than Ed's firewater. 🍺🍺🍺🍺

ROGUE MOGUL ALE

Oregon Brewing Co.
2320 OSU Drive
Newport, Oregon 97365
(503) 867-3660

Label Musings: Colorful, painted scene with a teal skier who is about to head down a steep slope. Colorful painted scene. He shouts, "Get real, get Rogue."

Colin: Approaches a stout: dark and heavy. The roasted malt flavor isn't bashful. A well-rounded effort. You may need some before you hit the bowls.
🍺🍺🍺

Randy: Ripe, feisty beverage that won't go down easily by itself. Match it with hearty, spicy food. Don't be foolhardy. Know your limitations, both on the slopes and at apres ski. A potent brew. 🍺🍺🍺

ROGUE ROGUE-N-BERRY ALE

Oregon Brewing Co.
2320 OSU Drive
Newport, Oregon 97365
(503) 867-3660

Label Musings: Violet painted bottle displays a sketch of a mellow, bearded hippie offering up a mug of green, glowing "Rogue." Deadheads are sure to approve.

Colin: Forgive me, but this beer wasn't berry, berry good to me. Most certainly an acquired taste. Life's too short for me to waste time trying to acquire tastes when there are so many beers out there that taste great from the get go. 🍺 ½

Randy: Who's that hippie callin' a Berry Head? I believe the label takes a pot shot at a certain ex-mayor of Washington, D.C. Also, what's that line on the back dedicating this beer to the "Pomerinke in each of us" supposed to mean? After a few brews I'm dizzy enough without the torture of trying to figure out riddles. Nothing special here, just another gimmicky fruit beer. 🍺 ½

ROGUE SHAKESPEARE STOUT

Oregon Brewing Co.
2320 OSU Drive
Newport, Oregon 97365
(503) 867-3660

Label Musings: The swashbuckler is back in blue, with burgundy lettering on a 22-ounce bottle.

Colin: When you pour a glass of this stuff, you'll swear you've struck oil. I guess the bookish types will go for this one. As for the answer to the question at hand: to drink, or not to drink? In my opinion, this stout is much ado about nothing. 🍺🍺

Randy: Ebony, chocolaty and oh, so rich. A keg, a keg, my kingdom for a keg! Definitely an imposing flavor. After one of these you may fall into a midsummer night's dream. 🍺🍺🍺

ROGUE ST. ROGUE RED ALE

Oregon Brewing Co.
2320 OSU Drive
Newport, Oregon 97365
(503) 867-3660

Label Musings: Red Rogue dude with a halo. Maybe he won it in a crap game.

Colin: I thought the canonization process was more stringent. Just the same, this is a rapturous bottle of ale. Serve it ice cold and you'll have a heavenly treat. 🍺🍺🍺 1/2

Randy: Bitter, spicy and robust. Not a mass-appeal brew and most certainly not saintly. I have always believed in the separation of church and beer. This brew may well even be unconstitutional. 🍺🍺

ROLLING ROCK BOCK

Latrobe Brewing Co.
Subsidiary of Labatt's USA
P.O. Box 350
Latrobe, Pennsylvania 15650
(412) 537-5545

Label Musings: The transparent label with a ram's head caught our attention. Plus, it's a natural with a name like "Rock Bock." But where is the "33"?

Colin: The ram on the label looks pretty pleased with himself and rightly so. Certainly, these brewers are pros. I'm sure they were concerned about adding this bock alongside their established winner. Not to worry. We can all delight that they took the plunge. Don't shy away from this bock. 🍺🍺🍺 ¹/₂

Randy: While popular demand has driven this brewery out of the micro class, this bock deserves mention because regular Rolling Rock is one of my all-time favorites. This is a bock beer for American tastes. It is lighter and crisper than most bocks, with little aftertaste. You can have more than one without feeling too full. I knew my pals from Latrobe wouldn't let me down. 🍺🍺🍺🍺

RUEDRICH'S RED SEAL ALE

North Coast Brewing Co.
444 North Main Street
Fort Bragg, California 95437
(707) 964-BREW

Label Musings: "Freak of nature" on the label: a giant, red seal perched on a rock. Call a team of marine biologists to take a look at this one. Maybe it was just some red dye no. 5 that leaked into the Pacific and wreaked havoc. Pretty weird.

Colin: I've never seen a red seal, but you might, after polishing off a 22-ounce bottle of this powerful ale. Trust me, you will get to the bottom. It's a quality ale from start to finish. 🍺🍺🍺 ¹/₂

Randy: Assertive and fulfilling ale. It may very well be the best ale you'll find with a red seal on the label. Granted, there's not much competition in that field. Good with some hearty grub. Toss me some raw fish. 🍺🍺🍺

SAMUEL ADAMS BOSTON ALE

Boston Beer Company
30 Germania Street
Boston, Massachusetts 02130
(617) 522-3400

Label Musings: Standard portrait of Sam on a
maroon background. The ingredients include Saaz,
Fuggles and Goldings hops. We can't say Fuggles with
a straight face. You try it.

Colin: It's hard to find fault with this one. If it's an ale
you crave, it stands up to the best. Although it has a
fairly bitter aftertaste, overall I'm not complaining.
🍺🍺🍺 ½

Randy: What can I say about this brewery without
being accused of fawning? It's smooth, even and
mellifluous. Let me make it simple for you: I like
Samuel Adams' beers. 🍺🍺🍺🍺

SAMUEL ADAMS BOSTON LAGER

Boston Beer Company
30 Germania Street
Boston, Massachusetts 02130
(617) 522-3400

Label Musings: Stoic patriot clasping a pewter stein.
Our founding fathers said it all: We are endowed with
certain inalienable rights, among them, life, liberty and
the pursuit of happiness. Beer does it for us. God
bless Sam and his ilk.

Colin: Simply a classic. Of course, who would expect
anything less from the legends up in Beantown. This is
the one you should buy to ease you through a Saturday
Yankees/Red Sox double-header on the tube. This is pure
genius in the art of beer making. Don't waste any more
time, hop on the bandwagon. 🍺🍺🍺🍺🍺

Randy: From one of the leading American
microbreweries. Their ads started to put the industry
on the map and we can all be grateful. This impec-
cable, flavorful lager is pristine. Advertising only goes
so far to sell your product if it doesn't deliver. You've
all probably tried this beer by now and know it's
damn good. 🍺🍺🍺🍺 ½

SAMUEL ADAMS CRANBERRY LAMBIC

Boston Beer Company
30 Germania Street
Boston, Massachusetts 02130
(617) 522-3400

Label Musings: Cranberry label framing our favorite patriot. Wasn't Sam the founding father who cried, "Give me good beer or give me death!" That man had guts.

Colin: On the sweet side, this novel effort didn't quite appeal to me. That cranberry taste; did they have to let it linger? If you want to reach outside the beer realm, I'd recommend one of the hard ciders that are increasingly crowding the beer shelves. Of course, Sam Adams' stalwarts will drink this one anyway. I can't blame them. The loyalty that the Beantown folks have engendered dies very hard. 🍺🍺

Randy: It is a fruit flavored wheat beer. Unless you're a devotee of fruit beers, especially those made with cranberries, I'd pass. Frankly, I tasted the cranberries only in the aftertaste. Stock up on it for Thanksgiving. It'll give everyone something to talk about. 🍺🍺

SAMUEL ADAMS CREAM STOUT

Boston Beer Company
30 Germania Street
Boston, Massachusetts 02130
(617) 522-3400

Label Musings: Sam's familiar portrait is sure to catch your eye; this time on a pewter background. According to Mr. James Koch, ale drinkers of Sam's day considered this brew "cream," while others were merely "milk."

Colin: The cream takes some of the bite out, but you're still firmly in stout territory. If you are a stout fan, by all means, give it a whirl. I recommend that everyone else stick to another one of Sam's gems. 🍺🍺🍺

Randy: Creamy is right! This stout is exceptional in its extraordinary smoothness and maltiness. Once again, this brewery has set a high standard for microbrewing. 🍺🍺🍺🍺

SAMUEL MIDDLETON'S PALE ALE

Wild Goose Brewery
20 Washington Street
Cambridge, Maryland 21613
(410) 221-1121

Label Musings: Old Sam Middleton clad in knickers and touting a walking stick stands proudly outside the state capitol building in Annapolis, Maryland. We think the colonial era bit belongs to Samuel Adams, but we like the green bottle.

Colin: Not a stand-out, but certainly noteworthy. Full of rich and bold flavor. If you're going to pack a case for a day of crabbing on the Chesapeake, this is an obvious choice. 🍺🍺🍺

Randy: I don't understand what this beer is trying to achieve. It is so bitter, it strikes me as just plain unpleasant. And I like to drink beer! Maybe it tastes better with crab cakes. 🍺

SANTA FE PALE ALE

Sante Fe Brewing Co.
P.O. Box 83, H.C. 75
Flying M Ranch
Galisteo, New Mexico 87540
(505) 988-2340

Label Musings: One of the sleekest labels you're likely to come across. Triangled, pastel portrait of a New Mexico landscape. Probably commissioned from a member of the high flying Santa Fe art scene. Hey, starving artists have to find a way to pay for their beer too. Neat yellow bottle cap is also a creative touch.

Colin: Pardon my forthrightness, but I found this beer to be rather unappealing. If you can't resist the pretty label, go ahead and buy a six-pack. Just don't get too curious about what's inside the bottle. 🍺

Randy: Full head and dark color. This attempt to marry the art world and the beer world may not appeal to either group. But, although it is rather unremarkable, it has that attractive label. Bring it to a party as an elegant conversation piece. 🍺🍺 ½

SARANAC ADIRONDACK AMBER LAGER

F.X. Matt Brewing Co.
811 Edward Street
Utica, New York 13502
(315) 732-3181

Label Musings: On Golden Pond. Green bottle with pale beige label, brown lettering and a peaceful, watercolored lake. Contributions from sales are made to the Adirondack Preservation Fund.

Colin: Its label proclaims this beer has a distinctive hop "memory," whatever that means. Actually, it's a fancy synonym for aftertaste. As for me, there's nothing memorable here, and I don't care how good the hop's memory is. This airy, flaccid lager does not have much of a body.

Randy: I found it to have a somewhat sour taste for a lager. A bitterness comes through in the aftertaste. Doesn't rate much praise. The Adirondacks aren't exactly the Rockies; this is the Adirondacks of beers. 1/2

SARANAC BLACK AND TAN

F.X. Matt Brewing Co.
811 Edward Street
Utica, New York 13502
(315) 732-3181

Label Musings: Mountain stream scene on black and tan label with brand name in bright orange letters. The color scheme works. Let's see if stout and lager mix is symbiotic.

Colin: Sorry to say, but this novel combination of stout and lager is schizophrenic. It's not sure what it's supposed to be and an unhappy marriage results. In the case of this blend, the whole is not as great as the sum of its parts.

Randy: As the label states, "It is a judicious melding" of stout and lager and has "multiple flavor notes." The smoothness is incredible for a brew this flavorful. For those who find straight stout too thick, sweet or overwhelming, look no further. Cutting it with lager is the ticket.

SARANAC GOLDEN PILSENER

F.X. Matt Brewing Co.
811 Edward Street
Utica, New York 13502
(315) 732-3181

Label Musings: The rustic setting will take you back to summer camp in the country. We've never been to the Adirondacks, but we guess this is what it looks like. Stately, colorful label reminded us of UCLA's uniforms: blue and gold.

Colin: It is hard to differentiate this insubstantial microbrew from the mass-produced brands. It is limp and lacking. I expect more from a microbrew. 🍺 ¹/₂

Randy: Ordinary, light golden pilsner with a very mild taste. If it's an extremely hot day and I'm in my garage working on my truck, I would appreciate this brew more. At best, it is refreshing. 🍺🍺

SARANAC SEASON'S BEST

F.X. Matt Brewing Co.
811 Edward Street
Utica, New York 13502
(315) 732-3181

Label Musings: Wintertime in the Adirondack Mountains graces this blithe label of a log cabin in the country. Even with all that snow on the ground, the familiar stream hasn't frozen over. Odd.

Colin: If this is the season's best, it couldn't have been a very good year. This celebration ale has a sour taste that lingers on and on. Pray for spring to be right around the corner. Then you can celebrate. 🍺🍺

Randy: Here's something different for the holidays. There's more of a barley flavor and it's less sweet or herbal than other special winter beers. Still, it's tasty and filling. Definitely a stocking stuffer. 🍺🍺🍺

SCHELL BOCK

August Schell Brewing Co.
P.O. Box 128
New Ulm, Minnesota 56073
(507) 354-5528

Label Musings: It's the standard issue bock ram, but a rather fine specimen. Somehow it is balanced on a barrel head. Must be a mini ram.

Colin: A bit on the mild side for a bock entry. Well-brewed, but if you want a bock, you probably would prefer a heartier version than what's offered here.
🍺🍺

Randy: This bock is sour and uninviting. The aftertaste overdoes it. It might be an acceptable accompaniment to a fine meal, but it doesn't stand up alone. 🍺 ½

SCHELL PILS

August Schell Brewing Co.
P.O. Box 128
New Ulm, Minnesota 56073
(507) 354-5528

Label Musings: An old saloon is depicted over a forest on this very professionally-done label. Those old-time drinkers look like they know their beer.

Colin: Smooth is the word that best captures this highly refined brew. If a mild, crisp beer is your style, this delicate pilsner from a very respected brewery easily fits the bill. 🍺🍺🍺 ½

Randy: Brewed since before the Civil War, this is an exceptional pilsner with lots of color and flavor. The aftertaste is slightly bitter, but overall it's a cultured glass of beer. 🍺🍺🍺

SCHELL WEIZEN

August Schell Brewing Co.
P.O. Box 128
New Ulm, Minnesota 56073
(507) 354-5528

Label Musings: An aesthetically pleasing label. Burnt orange "Schell" in script over painting of a pasture with interposed wheat field being plowed and a quail in flight. Excellent package for this premium brew.

Colin: Light and sweet, the perfect choice if you'd like to expose yourself to the wheat beer experience. A good antidote to summer swelter. The veterans at Schell have done an admirable job with this one. 🍺🍺🍺 ½

Randy: More carbonation and less wheat than I prefer in wheat beers. Nevertheless, it has a tangy flavor that not only sets it apart, but enables it to stand out. May be a little pricey for an experiment. 🍺🍺🍺

SCRIMSHAW PILSNER STYLE

North Coast Brewing Co.
444 North Main Street
Fort Bragg, California 95437
(707) 964-BREW

Label Musings: That poor whale looks like it's going down for the count. Maybe we can hook these guys up with the folks at Harpoon. Now that would be quite a party!

Colin: It has a significant level of taste for a pilsner, but retains the customary lightness and refreshing crispness. The result of the brewer's labors makes this one worth a taste. It comes in a big bottle, so get a friend and compare notes. 🍺🍺🍺

Randy: This flamboyant, hoppy pilsner is smooth and easy drinking. When you're out fishing, you may want to throw one back (beer that is), but beware, Moby Dick may want some payback. 🍺🍺🍺

SIERRA NEVADA BIGFOOT BARLEYWINE ALE

Sierra Nevada Brewing Co.
1075 East 20th Street
Chico, California 95928
(916) 893-3520

Label Musings: A friendly, bigfooted beast is humorously depicted hiding in the woods while a long-in-the-tooth prospector and his cowardly mule are petrified with fright. Gotta love that Bigfoot footprint on the cap.

Colin: Rich isn't the word. More than enough flavor for either a man or a beast. Be forewarned, you've got to be gutsy to go for this one. But if you think you can tackle it, give it a go. Sasquatch would be proud of this magnificent brew that bears one of his many nicknames. 🍺🍺🍺

Randy: Tastes like a Christmas ale. Full of hearty, unabashed flavor. Brewed using the barleywine process. You won't be able to drink more than a couple at a time. But after a few you may muster up enough courage (or be so bombed) that you'll want to venture into the deep brush to search for the mysterious beast yourself. 🍺🍺🍺 1/2

SIERRA NEVADA CELEBRATION ALE

Sierra Nevada Brewing Co.
1075 East 20th Street
Chico, California 95928
(916) 893-3520

Label Musings: A wreath wraps around a cozy winter cottage with its chimney going full blast. Would make a nice print for the den.

Colin: Sets the standard for holiday ales. You'll surely enjoy this truly special brew that is seasoned with just a hint of spice. Such a pity that Christmas comes but once a year. 🍺🍺🍺🍺 1/2

Randy: This fabulous, mellow ale is perfect for a celebration around holiday time. While 'tis true that it is much better to give than receive, I'd love someone to drop a case of this stuff under my Christmas tree. It would be a gesture of goodwill I wouldn't soon forget. 🍺🍺🍺🍺

SIERRA NEVADA PALE ALE

Sierra Nevada Brewing Co.
1075 East 20th Street
Chico, California 95928
(916) 893-3520

Label Musings: Picturesque mountain valley on a green label over a stocky, sturdy, short-nosed bottle.

Colin: Just the right amount of oomph for a member of the pale ale clan. The bitterness doesn't hide itself and neither does the aftertaste. You'll probably find it on your local supermarket shelf soon. 🍺🍺🍺

Randy: Fruitier than most of the pale ales. It has a "memory" that, unlike most, is pleasant and satisfying. But I'm not doing backflips; my doctor warned me about that. Since this one seems to be available at many supermarkets, I recommend you try it as an introduction to the world of microbrews. 🍺🍺🍺

SIERRA NEVADA PORTER

Sierra Nevada Brewing Co.
1075 East 20th Street
Chico, California 95928
(916) 893-3520

Label Musings: Standard stately Sierra Nevada label in pastel blue complete with the familiar babbling brook.

Colin: This is a strong-willed concoction. A stout seems to be hiding behind the porter label. As such, its audience will not be boundless. All in all, if you can face up to a brew on the rich end of the beer spectrum, you'll be pleased. 🍺🍺🍺 ½

Randy: Possesses sharper flavor than most porters, which can be watery despite their deep color. This is smooth and consistent. It is the best porter I sampled. Each of the Sierra Nevadas is an excellent rendition of its beer style. 🍺🍺🍺🍺 ½

SIERRA NEVADA STOUT

Sierra Nevada Brewing Co.
1075 East 20th Street
Chico, California 95928
(916) 893-3520

Label Musings: Standard Sierra Nevada mountain valley scene on a golden background. Remember to keep those colors straight because these styles of beers are quite different.

Colin: Although the label is full of sunshine, no rays of light will penetrate this stout. It hits you right up front. A dark hue and all the other formidable stout elements are present. Very tasty, if that's your cup of tea (or coffee). 🍺🍺🍺 ½

Randy: There is no question that this is stout. One sip and you realize you're up against a heavyweight. Its sweet yet burnt flavor distinguishes it from its British and Irish counterparts. Although this is fine brew, I don't believe it will garner a large audience. 🍺🍺🍺

SMITH & REILLY'S HONEST BEER

Smith & Reilly, Inc.
3107 N.E. 65th Street, No. E
Vancouver, Washington 98663
(206) 693-9225

Label Musings: They instruct you to serve it at 40-45 degrees. So do what you're told. The label is non-descript with green and white circular pattern on tan background. You can't accuse them of not being "honest" with their label boasts, there's hardly anything there.

Colin: It calls itself honest beer. Well, then it is entirely appropriate for me to give it to you straight. Mediocre, stilted and very dull are terms that best describe this uninspired beer. Honesty is a virtue, but it doesn't necessarily ensure good beer. 🍺 ½

Randy: Candidly, this all-malt brew doesn't supply much in the way of pleasing taste. I appreciate their veracity, but honestly, what were they thinking? I'd be lying if I were to tell you I enjoyed it. 🍺

SNOW CAP ALE

Hart Brewing, Inc.
P.O. Box 1179
Kalama, Washington 98625
(206) 673-2962

Label Musings: Snowcapped pyramid is an amusing touch. The black cap with red pyramid is neat as well. The label suggests it's best when served next to your favorite hearth after battling the rages of winter. It's almost poetic. Those brewers at Hart can really turn a phrase.

Colin: Rich and chocolaty, it's a hell of a winter warm up. Very filling. So skip the second piece of pie and have another one of these instead. Another reason to look forward to the holidays. 🍺🍺🍺🍺

Randy: Spicy, full-bodied winter warmer. Another fine brew from the consistently successful makers of the Pyramid line. They seldom make a misstep, and this is certainly not one of them. 🍺🍺🍺🍺 ½

SNOW GOOSE WINTER ALE

Wild Goose Brewery
20 Washington Street
Cambridge, Maryland 21613
(301) 221-1121

Label Musings: Colossal snow goose in flight over wintery terrain. Exceedingly sleek in black and white.

Colin: Only the most bitter of winter days could make you turn to this ale. While it has a hearty flavor, unfortunately it leaves a disagreeable finish. I think the goose on the label is heading south for the winter. 🍺🍺

Randy: Spicy like a winter ale but less syrupy than others. The usual sweetness is replaced here with bitterness. Try it only if you've got a curious streak. Which, after this, may turn into a mean streak. 🍺🍺

SPANISH PEAKS BLACK DOG ALE

Spanish Peaks Brewing Co. and Italian Cafe
P.O. Box 3644
Bozeman, Montana 59772
(406) 585-2296

Label Musings: "No whiners!" barks the label. Chug, the wonder dog, stands over snowcapped mountain peaks. Boy, talk about sucking up to the American beer-drinking public. They should go all the way and include fast cars and football players.

Colin: This is good stuff. Chug has earned his pedigree. Smooth, tasty, but not overpowering. This is going to make noise if it gets around. Beer drinkers won't tire of it quickly. My sincerest compliments to the folks at the cafe. 🍺🍺🍺🍺🍺

Randy: Smooth and sweet with a wheat beer flavor. Hey, where did those 22 ounces go? Spanish Peaks is in Bozeman, Montana. I'm buying a one-way ticket. I hope the pizza they serve at that Italian cafe is as good as the beer. 🍺🍺🍺🍺

SPANISH PEAKS BLACK DOG SWEETWATER WHEAT

Spanish Peaks Brewing Co. and Italian Cafe
P.O. Box 3644
Bozeman, Montana 59772
(406) 585-2296

Label Musings: Good ol' Chug the wonder dog. Somewhere up in Montana, that loyal companion is ready to welcome you to sample his hoppy wares.

Colin: A highfalutin', flavorful brew. Easy to drink with a very pleasing taste. There isn't a very detectable wheat flavor, if that is what you're after. Nevertheless, go fetch yourself some. 🍺🍺🍺 ½

Randy: Ah! I am picturing myself having a pizza at that Italian cafe in Bozeman, sipping this wonderful wheaty brew and petting my pal Chug. After a long day's work, one of these may be like having man's best friend bring you your slippers. And you don't have to take it for a walk. 🍺🍺🍺🍺

ST. STAN'S AMBER

St. Stan's Brewing Co.
821 L Street
Modesto, California 95354
(209) 524-4782

Label Musings: Green, mustard and white label pictures a plump monk hoisting an overflowing mug of brew. They call it "Alt" brew. No, they didn't forget the "M" for malt. It means it is a Dusseldorf-style dark beer.

Colin: A formidable, potent brew that's sure to put a dizzy grin on your puss. The tangy, syrupy taste wore on me after a while. Not worthy of sainthood, but pretty darn good.

Randy: As the label so eloquently describes, it is "[n]aturally pristine and pleasing to the palate." Plus, it's strong enough to knock your socks off. This fruity mixture of flavors is nicely balanced. Holy satisfying. 1/2

ST. STAN'S DARK

St. Stan's Brewing Co.
821 L Street
Modesto, California 95354
(209) 524-4782

Label Musings: Standard St. Stan's label scheme in rust, orange and tan. The inscription proclaims "conceived in heaven, brewed in California." Wow, it must be nice to have God on your side. With all those behemoth breweries dominating market share and retail shelf space, you need all the help you can get. Did you ever hear the story of David and Goliath?

Colin: Not the least bit subtle, this incredibly dark brew hits you with its force immediately. It's as delicious as it is strong. Obviously done with great care. Who says the California dream is dead? It's all right there in the bottle. 1/2

Randy: I found religion after sampling this tasty, caramel porter. Roasted, smooth and it keeps that wacky Friar Tuck on the label happy. 'Nuff said.

STARKE'S ORIGINAL HEAD HOG

Head Hog Brewing Co., Inc.
c/o Joseph Huber Brewing Co., Inc.
P.O. Box 277
1208 14th Avenue
Monroe, Wisconsin 53566
(608) 325-3191

Label Musings: A hog with an attitude dressed in an Indian headdress pictured inside a football. Why is this pig so angry? Maybe he'd prefer a ten-gallon hat instead.

Colin: It has an interesting, full flavor, falling a rung short of highest honors. With a little savvy marketing, it's sure to be a hit among all who are new to micros. Sure to be imbibed at college towns across the U.S.A. 🍺🍺🍺🍺

Randy: The label disclaims any affiliation with the N.F.L. Huh? Also, what is that "74" for? Don't be misled by the zany label, this is one serious brew. It has an even, gentle, wheaty taste. This hog goes to the head of the class. 🍺🍺🍺🍺

STEELHEAD EXTRA PALE ALE

Mad River Brewing Co.
P.O. Box 767
Blue Lake, California 95525
(707) 668-4151

Label Musings: Those of you with a lifetime subscription to Rod & Reel will love this one. Makes you want to break out the hip boots and lures and tie some flies.

Colin: I think they had a fishing trip in mind when they dreamed up this beauty. Sweet, crisp and extremely drinkable. Pack the Coleman lantern and a cooler of this stuff and you've got yourself an outing. Of course, you could just head down to the local beer joint and have a few. Either way, you are sure to be satisfied. 🍺🍺🍺🍺 ¹/₂

Randy: No fishiness here. It has a pale color, but don't let that fool you. I was hooked by its hearty, tangy lure. Amazing that such a translucent liquid can be so packed with flavor. A masterful job from the Mad River bunch. 🍺🍺🍺🍺

STEELHEAD EXTRA STOUT

Mad River Brewing Co.
P.O. Box 767
Blue Lake, California 95525
(707) 668-4151

Label Musings: Memorable scene of a steelhead trout hopping out of a stream. A prize catch for sure.

Colin: At first blush, it reminded me of unrefined crude oil. Actually, while unquestionably an acquired taste, you'll find it grows on you sip by sip. Even if you've never given stout a second thought, this well-crafted brew may be worth mustering up your courage for. 🍺🍺🍺🍺

Randy: The light blue label doesn't warn you of what is coming. What leaps out of the bottle is no trout, it's more like a sea monster. A smooth, creamy, coffee-like stout. If you know what you're in for, you'll be pleased. The Steelheads seem to give that little "extra" effort. 🍺🍺🍺🍺

TELLURIDE

Telluride Beer Co.
615 Rosetree Lane
Moab, Utah 84532
(801) 259-5210

Label Musings: Pastel view of a ski village scene. The streets are eerily deserted. Guess everyone's on the slopes or out at the saloons.

Colin: It is uniform in texture and has quite a bite. Might go well with a burger in the afternoon, but I wouldn't spend my night out drinking it. Telluwhat, take a pass. 🍺🍺

Randy: Light, pleasant, hoppy flavor, but it's potent enough to give you that buzz. Have a couple of these before hitting the slopes and the ski patrol will have your butt. 🍺🍺🍺

THOMAS KEMPER HEFE WEIZEN

Kemper Brewing Co.
22381 Foss Road N.E.
Poulsbo, Washington 98370
(206) 697-1446

Label Musings: Orange and purple background with glaring yellow lettering and wheat fields. Very colorful.

Colin: Not your usual wheat beer. Has a spunky flavor, unlike some of the duller tasting members of the variety. Extra points for originality. 🍺🍺🍺

Randy: This wheat beer struck me as sluggish. Its flavor was a disappointment. With all the great wheat beers out there, you can afford to be more choosey in your selections. 🍺🍺

THOMAS KEMPER INTEGRALE

Kemper Brewing Co.
22381 Foss Road N.E.
Poulsbo, Washington 98370
(206) 697-1446

Label Musings: Green, white and red flag over gold background. It must be Italy's colors, but this is America, ain't it? Break out the red, white and blue.

Colin: It is dark and spicy like a meatball, without much of a head. The slightly hoppy flavor doesn't pack much wallop. One is enough for me. A fairly unpleasant brew. What on earth does Integrale mean anyway? 🍺 1/2

Randy: Basta! Tastes like the last in a long series of beers over a full night's worth of "socializing." The aroma dredged up some scary flashbacks. Spare yourself. 🍺

THOMAS KEMPER PALE LAGER

Kemper Brewing Co.
22381 Foss Road N.E.
Poulsbo, Washington 98370
(206) 697-1446

Label Musings: Tidy blue pinstripe label with large yellow letters announcing "PALE LAGER."

Colin: Very disappointing effort by Mr. Kemper. I don't want to penalize creativity, but pale lagers should be light and refreshing. Unfortunately, this tasted bitter and sour. 🍺 ½

Randy: Surprisingly bitter for a lager, so I was caught off guard a little. Unless you want to sip a bitter drink to go with a nasty mood, stick with something more mellow. It's interesting that Thomas Kemper also carries a pilsner lager. 🍺🍺

THOMAS KEMPER PILSNER LAGER BEER

Kemper Brewing Co.
22381 Foss Road N.E.
Pousblo, Washington 98370
(206) 697-1446

Label Musings: Aqua background with glaring yellow lettering. Do labels sell beer or does the stuff in the bottle sell itself? Let's face it, some beers need all the help they can get to move off the shelf.

Colin: They call this a pilsner, but frankly I don't know where it properly belongs on the beer spectrum. Far from mild, so don't be misled. Stay clear if you're looking for a mellow, thirst quencher. 🍺

Randy: A sour and bitter pilsner? What gives? I don't see much appeal developing over this one. With all due respect, it is not a satisfying glass of beer. 🍺

THOMAS KEMPER WEIZEN BERRY

Kemper Brewing Co.
22381 Foss Road N.E.
Poulsbo, Washington 98370
(206) 697-1446

Label Musings: Raspberries accent this red label with large yellow letters. This is an all-malt lager flavored with raspberry juice.

Colin: Tastes like raspberry soda. However, it grows on you. It's surprisingly good and doesn't taste phony or watered down. Fruity and sweet. Have this novel beverage as a nice change of pace on a hot summer's day. 🍺🍺🍺🍺

Randy: Unmistakable, fruity flavor. There is real raspberry juice blended in. In my opinion, it's not just the best of the Thomas Kemper line, but perhaps the best American fruit-flavored beer. A very fine example of American ingenuity. 🍺🍺🍺🍺 ½

THOMAS POINT LIGHT GOLDEN ALE

Wild Goose Brewery
20 Washington Street
Cambridge, Maryland 21613
(410) 221-1121

Label Musings: Harmonious sketch of the Thomas Point Lighthouse at sunset. That crazy crab on the neck label and the trademark wild goose on the red bottle cap complete the look.

Colin: Smooth and very satisfying. This golden ale will put you in the mood for Maryland's famous sun and surf. Pack the cooler with this, break out the crab cakes and you'll have it made. 🍺🍺🍺 ½

Randy: Not a disagreeable brew, but I found it uneven and just a little too bitter. Crisp, but doesn't quite do the job. However, that crab sure does look tasty. 🍺🍺

TRADITIONAL BOCK

North Coast Brewing Co.
444 North Main Street
Fort Bragg, California 95437
(707) 964-BREW

Label Musings: The North Coast artists have come up with a fat, old goat to grace their bock entry. Looks like he's lost a step along the way. A glassy-eyed fuzz ball.

Colin: Wow! If it's flavor you crave, this potent brew will get your attention in a hurry. Clearly brewed with only serious bockers in mind, stay away unless you think you can handle it. Don't say I didn't warn you. 🍺🍺🍺 ½

Randy: Damn. I took one sip and my eyes crossed. No wonder that goat on the label looks slap happy. After a bottle of this bock, all the world's problems will seem to drift away. Good night. 🍺🍺🍺🍺

TRIPPEL TRAPPIST STYLE ALE

New Belgium Brewing Company, Inc.
350 Linden Street
Fort Collins, Colorado 80524
(303) 221-0524

Label Musings: Painting of three prancing nymphs. Or, depending on your perspective, three bombed, scantily-clad women playing ring around the rosy.

Colin: A cross between brandy and cough syrup. Certainly not ordinary, and not for me. Definitely potent at 7.5% alcohol content. No wonder those girls on the label are so giddy. What are Trappist monks doing making booze and hanging around with those tipsy gals anyway? 🍺🍺

Randy: Brewed with a special Belgian triple fermentation process. That's a mouthful. The result is very sweet and almost candy-like. Perhaps it may be the perfect choice for those who seek to mask a potent brew, but I don't encourage slipping anyone a micky. Add a cap for originality. 🍺🍺 ½

TUN TAVERN FOUNDERS' LAGER

Joseph Huber Brewing Co., Inc.
P.O. Box 277
1208 14th Avenue
Monroe, Wisconsin 53566
(608) 325-3191

Label Musings: Fabulous label celebrates Tun Tavern in Philadelphia, the birthplace of the Continental Marines. A portrait of the impressive Major Samuel Nicholas, First Commandant of the Marine Corps, is sketched on the neck label. Wonder if he oversees quality control at the great brewery in the sky.

Colin: From the Halls of Montezuma to the Shores of Tripoli, the Marines have earned the respect and admiration of a grateful nation. Now they have a beer they can call their own. Packs a formidable punch (just like your average Marine). The official beer of leathernecks everywhere. 🍺🍺🍺 ½

Randy: Medicinal, but it won't cure what ails you. Bitter like brussels sprouts. The armed forces bravely defend our shores and our freedoms. That includes the freedom to criticize this brew. Ah, the virtues of a free society. 🍺 ½

WASSAIL WINTER ALE

Full Sail Brewing Co.
506 Columbia Street
Hood River, Oregon 97031
(503) 386-2281

Label Musings: The Christmas trees must be huge in the Pacific Northwest. The snow-covered tree depicted on the label is a beaut.

Colin: It would have to be a cold winter's night indeed for most beer drinkers to appreciate this one. Thick, heavy and not the least bit subtle. You'll feel it going down. 🍺🍺

Randy: Bouillon with spices. Hearty and fulfilling. Don't go Christmas shopping after one of these. You'll feel so good (or be so looped) that your credit cards will be maxed out in no time. 🍺🍺🍺

WHEATHOOK ALE

The Redhook Ale Brewery
3400 Phinney Avenue North
Seattle, Washington 98103
(206) 548-8000

Label Musings: Garish, black label touts a bale of
wheat in a mug. The familiar trolleymen of Redhook
look like a real happy bunch.

Colin: This offering is sure to get you hooked on
wheat ale, if you're not there already. Robust with a
mellow aftertaste. Quite a brew. Just hop on the
trolley, pay your fare and don't forget the bottle
opener. 🍺🍺🍺 ½

Randy: Wheaty, slightly bitter and very delicious. A beer
lover's sure delight. Seattle certainly has become a mecca
for microbrewing. It's not just the home of Boeing, grunge
rock and Ken Griffey, Jr. anymore. 🍺🍺🍺🍺

WILD BOAR SPECIAL AMBER

Georgia Brewing Co.
P.O. Box 8239
Atlanta, Georgia 30306
(404) 633-0924

Label Musings: One mean pig staring down at you.
Rob and Bob boast, "The best amber beer in America."
Them's fightin' words, but this brew was an award
winner at the Great American Beer Festival.

Colin: That pig means business. This amber ale has
all the wallop its name would suggest. Quiche eaters
need not apply. This is a strong and flavorful brew. I
admire brewers with the guts to give it to us straight.
🍺🍺🍺🍺 ½

Randy: My first reaction was, "Whoa, baby!" There is
so much flavor here it's baffling. Is it fruity or flowery
or sweet or bitter? Other critics would simply say it's
complex. I can see how professional judges might be
impressed, but my palate isn't a computer. This beer
will not attract a large audience. 🍺🍺 ½

WILD GOOSE AMBER

Wild Goose Brewery
20 Washington Street
Cambridge, Maryland 21613
(410) 221-1121

Label Musings: Wild geese and the Chesapeake crab on a bright green bottle. You gotta love that marine wildlife, especially on a plate. With a couple of tall, cold ones, of course.

Colin: A solid effort by the folks in Maryland, but they overdid it just a tad. The average beer fan will likely prefer a less potent brew. Just the same, sample one while standing in the long lines at Camden Yards waiting for O's tickets.

Randy: Bitter! An overpowering pinch of flavor gooses you but good. Not for the faint-hearted. Don't say I didn't tell you so. You make the call.

WIT!

Spring Street Brewing Company, Inc.
225 Lafayette Street
New York, New York 10012
(212) 226-9110

Label Musings: Funky, artsy design with a distinct, red exclamation point that will grab your attention.

Colin: This brew was created by a former hot shot Wall Street lawyer. Do you still want to try some? The flavor has a hint of fruit and a satisfying sweetness. I killed a six-pack. Maybe he can get me off easy.

Randy: This is a white wheat beer, similar to Celis White. The recipe supposedly dates back to 1444. One would think brewing techniques would have improved in the last 550 years. Too much fruitiness and a cologne-like smell. It might be good at brunch, but I'd rather have a mimosa. 1/2

WOODCHUCK DRAFT CIDER AMBER

Joseph Cerniglia Winery
RFD #1, P.O. Box 119A
Proctorsville, Vermont 05153
(802) 226-7575

Label Musings: That nutty woodchuck is about to gnaw into a big, crisp apple. If you look closely, you'll see his name "Marmota monax monux." Can any Latin speakers out there translate for us?

Colin: If your usual bitter or sour tasting brew has become a bit tired, try this sweet, light alternative. You'll be tempted to guzzle, but try to sip. It should be savored and its hefty alcohol content must be kept in mind. This ain't soda pop, folks. It's a lot better. 🪙🪙🪙🪙

Randy: Super-sweet apple cider. Hey wait, I'm bombed. You won't know what hit you until it does, and then it'll be too late to stop. This is creative stuff. Is it OK if I pass out now? 🪙🪙🪙🪙

WOODCHUCK DRAFT CIDER DARK & DRY

Joseph Cerniglia Winery
RFD #1, P.O. Box 119A
Proctorsville, Vermont 05153
(802) 226-7575

Label Musings: We know it's not beer, so relax. We just thought you might want to know what it tastes like, that's all. Besides, it's in the beer section isn't it? Wild, untamed woodchuck graces the label. Are the folks that made this playing on the name of the Woodpecker Cider famous over in England? They say it's been made in the Green Mountains for over 400 years. Boy, even back then Americans loved a little pick me up.

Colin: Imagine apple juice combined with vinegar and you can see why this concoction isn't for everybody. Of course the folks in Vermont are a breed apart. However, it is zesty and undeniably original. You may go for it. 🪙🪙 ¹/₂

Randy: Looks like soda pop in the mug and tastes like apple cider. It's definitely not a beer, if that's what you're after. The amber is much sweeter; the dark and dry is considerably more sour. Just a historical note. Unless the brewers mean Native Americans or explorers, there were no settlements in America 400 years ago. 🪙🪙

YUENGLING PORTER

D.G. Yuengling & Son Inc.
P.O. Box 539
5th & Manhantongo Street
Pottsville, Pennsylvania 17901
(717) 622-4141

Label Musings: American eagle gripping a keg o'
beer on a red label that proclaims it's from America's
oldest brewery, since 1829. To keep brewing beer
through so many wars and depressions (not to
mention surviving Prohibition), they've got to be
good.

Colin: Some will find this porter hard to distinguish
from a stout, other than the lack of aftertaste. Stout
lovers should definitely put this one on their list. All
others may not want to tread on this territory. I don't
mean to knock this assertive brew, but it's surely not
for everyone. 🍺🍺🍺

Randy: Like many other porters, it is opaque and
thin with a burnt, woody flavor. This one is ordinary
and non-descript. Don't get me wrong, it is potent
enough. After a couple of these, those 6-10 spares
won't be gimmees. 🍺🍺

YUENGLING TRADITIONAL LAGER

D.G. Yuengling & Son Inc.
P.O. Box 539
5th & Manhantongo Street
Pottsville, Pennsylvania 17901
(717) 622-4141

Label Musings: America's oldest brewery strikes
again with the bald eagle, green bottle and gold cap.
You have to respect those veteran small breweries.
Their steadfastness has paved the way for the rebirth
of microbreweries from coast to coast.

Colin: Although the Yuenglings have been around for
a long time, they haven't gotten it right yet, at least not
with this one. Light, watery and not too appealing. I
found it to be a rather mediocre lager. 🍺🍺

Randy: I believe this is an up-to-the-mark lager. It is
capable of developing a following if distributed nationally.
You should taste a mass-produced brand, then one of
these and see which you like better. 🍺🍺🍺

— A —

— B —

— C —

— D —

— E —

— F —

— I —

— J —

— K —

— L —

— M —

— S —

— T —

— W —

— Y —